The New America

POLITICS AND SOCIETY IN

Basic Books, Inc. NEW YORK

The New America

THE AGE OF THE *Smooth Deal*

BY Karl E. Meyer

FOR *Sarah*

Let it be clear that this Administration recognizes
the value of daring and dissent—that we greet
healthy controversy as the hallmark of healthy change.

Contents

The New America

The Fallen Idol

INAUGURAL EVE, 1961. On the last day of the Eisenhower Administration, there was a mood of zestful impatience in Washington. An old and tired man was about to be supplanted by the youngest President ever elected—and even among Republicans it was felt that the talisman of youth was needed. The Capital had wearied of Eisenhower the Just, his stumbling speeches, his retinue of cronies, his grin. In the last days, it was as if his Administration had ceased to exist; the wits in the salons had stopped joking about the General. The incoming President, and his flamboyant family, was fresher material.

The snow came, covering the city in a spotless mantle. The symbolism was not lost—this was the New Frontier, the rebirth that everyone wanted. Yet there was little sentimentality in the air; Washington's favorite adjective—so the *New Republic* informs us—is "tough." Politics is an uncharitable calling, and Washington is the least charitable of cities. The word "dead" describes an outcast politician, and the terrible finality of the term was now applied to Mr. Eisenhower.

Amid the jubilation, a thoughtful observer might well have asked what really had changed. Would a new man in the White House make that much difference? In a city so given to tough-mindedness, could it be that on this most important question the fashionable view was suffused with delusion? In short, was it not possible that President Eisenhower had been made a scapegoat and had been saddled with the faults of his fellows in order that the tribe might lessen its sense of guilt?

In the usual indictment, the first count against Mr. Eisenhower was that he failed to use the power of his office but remained a bemused spectator of events. But what about the leaders of the opposition party on Capitol Hill? Could it honestly be said that they had been bold, intrepid spirits, exercising their influence to the full? Isn't it fairer to say that on many vital points the Democrats in Congress were as cautious and passive as the President they refused to criticize by name?

The second count against Mr. Eisenhower was that he relied heavily on the black arts of Madison Avenue, and substituted public relations for leadership. But were the leaders of the opposition strangers to the devices of polling and of hidden persuasion? Or wasn't the real complaint, more often than not, that the Republicans were able to raise more money for their sales campaigns than the Democrats?

The third count was that Mr. Eisenhower was indifferent to ideas and placed fiscal orthodoxy above national need. But could it be plausibly maintained that the floor of Congress was electric with imaginative proposals? In terms of fiscal policy, wasn't it true that the Democratic leadership in Congress at several critical points boasted of its economizing skill and sought to outplay the President at his own game of thrift?

In sum, would a change in the White House bring a change in substance—or only in style? Among the celebrants on Inaugural Eve, there were some sceptics who feared that the habits and attitudes that had come to predominate in the past decade would blight the promise of Mr. Kennedy's New Frontier. Specifically, they were concerned about the cult of slickness in politics—in which, carried to its logical extreme, issues become slogans, leadership becomes play acting, and the means of politics an end in themselves.

It is this legacy that provides my theme. In examining it, I do not pretend to be fair—only candid. My aim is to apply a little sandpaper to our political icons, liberal and conservative. If sometimes I seem to rub a bit too hard, it is not out of malice but out of a desire to contribute in a small way to the vitality of a society in which it frequently appears that "moderation" is being practiced to excess.

Part One / Symptoms

1 /

The Taming of American Politics

> Most every American likes to be entertained. He likes
> the movies; he likes mysteries; he likes fireworks and
> parades. He likes Jack Benny and Bob Hope and
> Joe E. Brown!
> So if you can't fight, PUT ON A SHOW! And if you put on
> a good show, Mr. and Mrs. America will turn out
> to see it.
>
> —CLEM WHITAKER, *California Political Counselor*

THE GREAT PRESIDENTIAL ELECTION of 1960 was
the first that television won. Never before had two nominees been so concerned with cameras and cosmetics, and
seldom had the voters been so fascinated by politics-as-
theater. Midway in the great debates, *Time* complained
that "increasingly, people seem to be judging the debating
as theatrical performances," and Joseph Alsop remarked
laconically on the "extraordinary, openly panicky scenes"
enacted in Washington in preparation for the second television encounter. "Grandees of the Republican Party,"
Mr. Alsop wrote, "spent days arguing about the techni-
calities of lighting, the effects of different kinds of back-
drop, and the drawbacks and advantages of different kinds

of pancake makeup. Nothing quite like this has ever been seen before in American politics."

But the theatrics tended to distract attention from some important offstage changes that lay behind the close victory of President John F. Kennedy. Not only did the victor and the vanquished owe a formidable debt to television, but the campaign also marked the culmination of many less obvious developments in our politics. In the broadest sense, the election signified that a new generation, using novel political techniques, was assuming leadership of a country vastly different from the land our forefathers knew.

I I

The 1960 Presidential election in many ways summed up and symbolized the changes that have taken place in American life. Compare it, for example, to the election a century before, won by Abraham Lincoln, a frontier-born lawyer who was practically a stranger to Washington.

A hundred years ago, the world outside was only a witness to our campaign, not a participant. In 1960, as if to underline the change, a score of foreign rulers were on the soil of New York in the midst of the election. One national candidate was the grandson of the Senator famous as the nemesis of the League of Nations, and the Democratic nominee was the son of an equally well-known Massachusetts isolationist. Yet so far as concerns foreign policy, Mr. Lodge and Mr. Kennedy had more in common with each other than either had with the views of his illustrious forebears.

In 1860, the Union was on the verge of dissolution. But the passage of a hundred years carried the country to the opposite shore, in which many thinking men were more concerned with the excess of *unum* rather than *pluribus*. The decline of regionalism, of ethnic pluralism, and of dissident minorities—these tendencies raised new fears of a nation *too* closely bound by the invisible chords of radio and television.

The political parties of Lincoln's day were, to the nation's misfortune, divided on a matter of fundamental principle. But in 1960, the area of agreement between the two national platforms and the four national candidates was remarkable. Even on the question of race, both parties adopted "strong" civil rights planks; Dixie did not secede from the Democracy; and the official Southern candidate for the Presidential nomination was a Texan who presided over the passage of the first civil rights laws since Reconstruction times.

Lincoln's America was an alliance of proud and quarrelsome states, and Washington, D.C., was regarded by many as the lair of Satan. Ten decades later, every active candidate for the Presidential nomination was a job-holder in Washington (Richard M. Nixon, John F. Kennedy, Hubert Humphrey, Stuart Symington, and Lyndon B. Johnson), and the subsequent tickets were composed of four men who *all* rose to prominence from the U.S. Senate. For good measure, both national party chairmen were, for the first time, Senators too.

In 1860, the vote was sectional; Lincoln failed to carry a single Southern state. A century later, the two major parties were more nearly national than ever before. Even the most persistent one-party enclaves—including South Carolina and Maine—were battlegrounds in the Presidential campaign. Equally striking was the eclipse of the local political bosses who in Lincoln's day controlled national conventions. Television had created a new constituency which overleaped the boundaries of the precinct —and the camera eye had a devastating effect on the convention's secluded, smoke-filled rooms.

A century ago, the Presidential ballot contained four parties, every one of which received an appreciable portion of the vote. By 1960, the United States had become a two-party nation, with a vengeance. For the first time since its founding, the Socialist Party withdrew altogether from the Presidential battle; the vote for minor-party candidates fell to an all-time low. The country was too distracted to notice, but in 1960 the United States became the only Western democracy in which minor party dissent was virtually inaudible.

Finally, though the country was young in 1860, the symbols of age and gravity were considered appropriate to political leadership. After his election to the Presidency at the age of 52, Lincoln began to grow a beard, and six of the seven Presidents who succeeded him wore hirsute adornment. A hundred years later, the youngest pair of contenders were nominated for President at the very moment our oldest Chief Executive presided in the White House. Significantly, it was the first time that both major-party nominees were born in the twentieth century.

I I I

All of these contrasts reflect the institutional changes which have altered America and have made a profound difference in where, how, and why we live. The most readily apparent change is that as a nation we have moved from the farm to the city. A century ago, four-fifths of our population lived in rural areas; today, the figure has been emphatically reversed. Not only do the vast majority of Americans live in urban areas, but according to *Fortune*, forty million persons live in communities that can be called "strictly suburban."

The inevitable interdependence of city living has affected our whole pattern of life. Economically, the farmers and artisans of Lincoln's America enjoyed a high degree of self-sufficiency; nowadays, we are a nation of hired men. It is estimated that 38 per cent of the working force is employed in organizations that have over 500 employees. The organizational web binds even the professional man and the small entrepreneur, whose livelihood is directly affected by Big Business, Big Labor, and Big Government.

City life tends to lessen traditional rural prejudices, and today the old bigotries which used to fence people apart are being leveled. It scarcely caused a ripple of comment when a member of the Jewish faith was elected Governor of Connecticut, and another became Senator from Oregon; even the Negroes are reaching the outer fringes of the power elite. Ethnically, we are nearly all (95 per cent) American born, and 80 per cent of the population is of third-generation stock. The most obvious sign of the change is that a Roman Catholic who is a descendant of Irish immigrants now sits in the highest office of the land.

In both city and suburb, the contrast between rich and poor has diminished. Although residual poverty still persists, it is fair to say that more Americans are better off than ever before. Some 43 per cent of all non-farm families have an after-tax cash income of between $5,000 and $10,000. Without succumbing to complacent self-congratulation, Americans can be rightfully impressed by the estimate that nearly a third of all college-age youngsters will be enrolled on a campus by 1970.

Lincoln's America was decentralized and sparsely settled. Today, the jet plane has shrunk the physical distance, and the vacuum tube the cultural distance, in a country that has closed the frontier. The chief organs of public opinion in 1860 were the brash local newspapers and the boisterous political meetings. But the press is no longer so brash or competitive, and the little black box in the living room has supplanted the rallies.

In nations as well as individuals, however, success can lead to lassitude and lack of purpose. The very closeness of the election suggested that whatever Mr. Kennedy's intentions, the nation was not yet in a very adventurous mood. In 1960, a year of epochal change elsewhere in the world and a time of decision in the United States, the typical titles of best-sellers were *Enjoy, Enjoy!*, *The Good Years*, and *How I Made $2,000,000 in the Stock Market*.

I V

If we were to sum up the differences between elections past and present, it could be said that the United States had moved from the politics of the country store to the politics of the supermarket. The old-time country store was local, individualistic, homely, inefficient—and pungently aromatic. The modern supermarket is a national institution, standardized, glamorous, superbly efficient—and notably deodorized. In 1960, our two living ex-Presidents, Herbert Hoover and Harry Truman, seemed like nostalgic remnants of the era of the country store. Their style of politics was several light years removed from that of the two clean-shaven young men who stepped briskly into and out of the shopping centers.

During the campaign, it often seemed as if the country were caught in a sales war between Safeway and the A & P. Even the language of politics was affected; the key words we recall were "image," "format," "exposure," and "prestige"—the argot of Madison Avenue. Although President Eisenhower had been nationally merchandised in 1952 and 1956, this was the first time both candidates rifled the stockroom of supermarket politics.

In supermarket politics, four approaches are evident: (1) the candidate is looked upon as a product; (2) the campaign is regarded as a promotion drive; (3) issues are considered "themes"; and (4) political leadership is regarded as primarily a matter of managerial *expertise*. Let us examine what this means to the consumer, *i.e.*, the voter,

(1) *The candidate as a product.* The classic statement of this viewpoint was offered by Rosser Reeves, a partner in the advertising firm of Ted Bates & Co., and creator of the "Eisenhower Answers America" spot campaign in 1952. "I think of a man who hesitates between two levers as if he were pausing between competing tubes of toothpaste in a drugstore," Mr. Reeves explained. "The brand that has made the highest penetration on his brain will win his choice, and the nature of the human brain is such that a one-minute or thirty-second speech, expertly crystallized, gets a maximum penetration on its content."

Although it was something of a shock in 1952 to find the body politic clothed in gray flannel, the ethos by 1960 had become familiar. Midway in the campaign, Joseph Alsop lamented: "To date, in truth, a good deal of the private comment on this campaign has suggested that Presidential candidates are like dogfood. The packaging has got all the attention; the contents of the package far too little."

(2) *The campaign as a promotion drive.* As a corollary

of (1), the first step in a campaign is to analyze the product and cold-bloodedly contrast its strengths and weaknesses with the competing brand. Polls and surveys are invaluable in determining the "image" the candidate must project, and then work must be begun long before election day. "I believe most aspirants for public office start much too late," John F. Kennedy has written. "When you think of the money that Coca-Cola and Lucky Strike put into advertising day after day, even though they have well-known brand names, you can realize how difficult it is to become an identifiable public figure."

If the drive is going to clinch the sale, an effective organization must be formed well in advance. The party machine is not enough. Special "volunteer" groups supplement the regular party cadres, and a variety of committees are established for veterans, farmers, union members, doctors, lawyers, and Hollywood stars. A successful politician will also develop a personal organization that can bypass formal party leaders. The task is formidable; after the Los Angeles convention, Robert F. Kennedy announced: "We're trying to get an organization going that is bigger than U.S. Steel, and we're trying to do it in three months."

(3) *The issue as a "theme."* After the candidate has been selected, what is the next thing to be considered? The shrewdest answer comes from Murray Chotiner, dean of the supermarket strategists and erstwhile campaign manager to Richard M. Nixon:

> It is the theme of the campaign. I have never believed in a slogan for a campaign. The reason is, so many times the opposition may twist it or turn it. You can have a theme without a slogan. And the theme should restrict the issues to two, instead of trying to cover the entire waterfront.

That doesn't mean that you should not be prepared, if necessary, to answer questions that may be presented. But you cannot campaign on a multitude of issues. You will be able to sell no more than two or three issues at the outside.

As an example of a successful theme, Mr. Chotiner cites the cases of Congressman Donald Jackson of California, who is a member of the House Committee on Un-American Activities. The theme was taken from something George Washington said: "Put none but Americans on guard tonight." Mr. Jackson became known as the "on guard for America man" for his vigilance in ferreting out subversive Hollywood extras.

Once the theme is established, the candidate reiterates it over and over again in speeches carefully processed for audience reaction. Mr. Nixon was especially notorious for this practice; reporters called his standard, pretested utterance, "The Speech." Even the Vice President's celebrated acceptance speech in Chicago was, as William Shannon pointed out, "little more than an anthology of favorite selections, dating back to 1954." And, like a good television commercial, this speech was a skillful combination of repetition, simplicity of statement, identification with glamour, and appeals to homely sentiment.

(4) *The politician as a managerial expert.* Obviously, the man who can best handle these chores is not one with deep beliefs who might risk offending the consumer by pushing an unpopular theme. Ideally, the perfect candidate is a person with a projectable image on television, with skills in organization and selling, and with a minimum of ideological baggage. Many of the same qualities that go into a successful corporate executive now are sought out in politics.

There was at least one striking similarity between Mr. Kennedy and Mr. Nixon—both men wound up in politics as much through chance as decision. Mr. Nixon has freely confessed that if Cromwell & Sullivan had offered him a job after graduation, "I am sure I would be there today, a corporation lawyer instead of Vice President." And in an essay entitled "Why Go Into Politics," Mr. Kennedy has written:

> . . . I never thought in school and college that I would ever run for office myself. One politician in the family was enough, and my brother Joe was obviously going to be that politician. I hadn't considered myself a political type. . . . My brother Joe was killed in Europe as a flier in August, 1944, and that ended our hopes for him. But I didn't even start to think about a political profession until more than a year later.

At the outset, neither man was particularly committed to any set of political convictions; although both were in college during the New Deal era, neither was caught up in the passions of the time. *Time* quotes Mr. Kennedy as saying: "In my family we were interested not so much in the ideas of politics as in the mechanics of the whole process."

Thus, in 1960, the American people had to choose between two candidates who, except for accident and circumstance, might have wound up in the other's party, or in one of the sprawling business organizations that now set the tone of American life.

V

In the supermarket, however, the test of success is sales; in politics more subtle standards prevail. Norman Thomas, though he never won an election, has had considerably more influence on our political life than scores of politicians who never lost. No doubt there have always been political leaders who were more pitchmen than prophets. What is cause for concern is the disappearance of those who did bring purposeful zeal to the business of politics.

The uncomfortable fact is that much of the world is nearer to the America of 1860 than to the affluent land of the present. It is not the mechanics but the ideas of politics that have caught the imagination of the emerging masses of Asia, Africa, and Latin America. Perhaps the most symbolic episode of the whole 1960 campaign was the simultaneous meeting of the United Nations General Assembly in New York. The contrast could not have been greater between the two Presidential candidates and the flamboyant foreign leaders who arrived on our shore. Khrushchev, Nasser, Gomulka, Nkrumah, Tito, Castro, Nehru, and Sukarno—all of them deeply committed men, most of whom had served in prison for their political beliefs. It is with these men, and the world they represent, that the Kennedy Administration must deal.

Fortunately, Mr. Kennedy shows promise of being something far better than a supermarket politician. It is superfluous to add that he displayed a verve of manner, a toughness of mind, and a sense of history in his campaign. The question is how long the spurt of enthusiasm will last before Washington returns to its accustomed diet of instant inertia. Will Kennedy govern the Capital, or will the Capital govern Kennedy?

2 /

Washington: Leviathan, Inc.

> They see visions of great cities and wild regions; they
> are in the marts of commerce, or amid the islands of
> the South; they gaze on Pompey's pillars or on the Andes;
> and nothing which meets them carries them forward or
> backward, to any idea beyond itself.
>
> —JOHN HENRY NEWMAN

THE CONVENTIONAL SYMBOLS of Washington,
D.C., according to the guide books, are the White House,
the Capitol, and the Washington Memorial. But to those
who are interested in the inner life of our Capital City,
three other symbols are perhaps far more meaningful:
the Robotyper, the executive desk, and the film clip.

I intend no frivolity. The vaulting monuments, the
marble halls, and the stately Executive Mansion—these
are indeed proud emblems of our National Capital. But
they provide the format—to use an increasingly popular
word—for our political pageant. Far more intriguing to
the close-hand observer is the machinery hidden behind
the stage—the apparatus which help to determine the en-
trances and exits in the one drama that Washington finds
all-absorbing.

Let us see how these devices work:

Item. A constituent opens his mailbox, and is surprised to find a letter from Senator J. Standard Blankhead extending congratulations on the birth of a new baby. Our voter is pleased and flattered that amidst his busy rounds Mr. Blankhead found time to dictate and sign a personal note concerning an intimate family event. In his glow of good feeling, it is probably for the best that our voter remains ignorant of the roomful of machinery that processed a letter virtually untouched by human hands.

Item. Subsequently, our constituent visits Washington in order to see the Director of an important Government agency. He is duly impressed by the wall-to-wall carpeting, the expansive walnut desk, and the soothing decor in the office occupied by the Director. What he does not realize is that every item—down to the water carafe, telephone table, and lowly ash tray—is determined by formal rituals that would be the envy of a tribal chieftain in the most tradition-oriented culture of Borneo.

Item. Home again, our voter snaps on the television set and sees his Congressman in a question-and-answer interview with an important Cabinet officer. But happily for the Congressman, the constituent does not know that the interview never took place. It is the result of some clever splicing of two film clips: one of the Cabinet official answering a series of carefully prepared questions; and the other of the Congressman reading the questions.

These details of the conduct of our democracy would be trivial if they were not so symptomatic of a basic condition of Washington: the almost obsessive concern with the mechanics of government, as against the purposes of government. We shall explore the implications of this fact later, but first let us take a Cook's Tour into the obscurer corners of democracy's national headquarters.

II

Our tour begins in the arcanum of the Capitol, in the network of subterranean corridors that link the halls of Congress. One passageway, near the Senate subway, has little to distinguish it in any outward manner—and yet its doors conceal one of the most intriguing sights on Capitol Hill. Known as the "Robotyper rooms," this small area is the source of most of the mail that floods each day into the Senate postal station.

Never before have our Senators been so conscious of the power of the pen. Postal officials calculate that on a typical day about 15,000 assorted pieces of mail flow from the Senate into the belt-driven conduits in the basement. In December, the Yuletide sentiment swells the daily outpouring to about 20,000 pieces. The volume is steadily increasing; according to postal authorities, the amount of mail has increased about 15 per cent in the last two years.

In short, Congress has become one of the country's most potent direct-mail advertisers. Part of the credit for this is surely due to Senator Russell B. Long of Louisiana, who on a historic day not long after World War II is credited with introducing the first six Robotypers.

Specialists regard these first machines as somewhat primitive. They work something like this: a punched roll resembling the old player-piano roll is coupled to a typewriter. But instead of Chopin, a form letter emerges, impeccably typed in the blue ink customary on Capitol Hill. However, a stenographer must manually append the date, heading and salutation—and the Senator might be called upon to sign his name.

The subsequent arrival of the Friden Flexowriter Automatic Writing Machine added new refinements to the art. This device, more intricate and "sophisticated," feeds on a thin roll of punched pink tape which must be "programmed" for a specific task. One tape can handle the body of a letter, while another can reproduce a list of names. Thus a tape properly programmed can eliminate any manual typing. The newest model—a Duplex Flexowriter—combines the two operations by perfectly coordinating the tapes. The resulting spectacle is awesome; an operator needs only to watch while stationery is automatically fed into the Flexowriter and emerges flawlessly typed, from the "October 3, 1960" to the "SD/elm" at the bottom.

Only the Senator's signature needs to be added. For this purpose, an Autopen has been invented—a formidable-looking machine about the size of a spinet but of more limited virtuosity. The Senator's signature is coded on a large drum which drives an actual pen in a holder, reproducing the name down to the last squiggle and dot. Care must be taken not to feed in letters too hastily, or the pen will vibrate and create a palsied effect fatal to the image of Congressional vigor.

Envelopes, too, can be automatically addressed, or a window envelope can be used which allows the Flexo-written address to peek through. Then, up to the mechanical stuffing machine and automatic sealer and presto! a mass mailing is ready to be spilled down the mail tube to the postal conveyor belts.

Who gets the letters? It depends. If the Senator is a stick-in-the-mud, only those constituents who actually write to his office. When mail on a specific question has reached sufficient volume (usually around 25 letters), then a form response is programmed for the machines below. But if the Senator is more enterprising, his staff will secure the names of graduating high school seniors, and the marriage and birth listings in the local newspapers. Then a mass mailing will extend personalized congratulations. A sample letter—this is a composite of a half-dozen the author has seen—will run something like this:

> Congratulations on your new boy! Since my wife and I have seven children, we are all too familiar with the problems of a growing family. When we learned of your happy event, we thought that you might like to know that the Department of Agriculture has prepared a helpful booklet entitled "Infant Care." Clara and I would be delighted to send you a copy if you drop us a note.

The pulse of politics governs the mailing campaign; in an election year—or at graduation time—the demand may be too great for the Senator's own Robotyper room. The overflow will be handled in a Robotyper pool available to all members. As of last October, there were about a hundred machines in the pool, but the size increases steadily since outgoing Senators leave their machines to the common cause of staying in office.

Meanwhile, lobbyists too have mastered the arts of mechanical mailings. Thus a Senator may be deluged by mail from auto salesmen or undertakers opposing this or that legislation—and all the letters are electronically processed. The Senator then prepares a standard answer, which again is fed into the Robotypers—meaning that machines are talking to machines, with the postman's thumbprint adding the only human touch. But doubtless in a few years those fully automated post offices will take care of *that*.

III

We turn now from the legislative to the executive, and our first stop is the Department of Agriculture, which has spilled over into two buildings astride Independence Avenue. Inside, we find ourselves in one of the interminable corridors that form the capillaries of modern government. Plain wood doors are spaced every twelve feet, and next to the doors there are small placards containing the cryptic glyphs which identify the officials within.

To the casual visitor, it seems as if identical doors must open into no less tediously uniform offices. Hardly so.

We enter the suite of one of the Department's Branch Chiefs—he is a GS-14, or a level below the first rung of the executive. However, our man is a Chief, therefore he is entitled to a private office. But it is a dowdy, poor thing. It is furnished in what the trade calls "Contemporary Federal," *i.e.*, a dull gray steel. The fixtures seem metallic and somber, including the steel coat rack and the plastic ash tray which sits on a dun-colored desk. The badly hung pictures on the wall are blowups of photographs taken by the WPA years before. In a cubicle walled by a glass partition, the Chief's secretary works in cramped quarters overflowing with file cabinets and reams of paper. Her heelless shoes clump on a dirty brown linoleum floor.

So dwells a GS-14 in his melancholy cell of rivets and rawness. But directly across the hall is the office of the Deputy Director, who is a GS-15, just a digit higher. Walking into his reception room, one has a feeling of serenity and spaciousness. A lovely tweed broadloom runs from wall to wall and forms a soft path into the inner office. Within, the Deputy Director is seated at a large walnut desk with an inlaid conference table adjoining it. Leather-padded chairs, with brass studs, are scattered around the table; the ash trays are of round amber glass set in a walnut base. The difference in status has even wrought cosmetic miracles on the secretarial help. Seated before her new electric typewriter, the Deputy Director's Secretary is noticeably more chic in dress, more brisk in manner, than the Girl Who Works for a GS-14. A walnut in-box and a leather swivel chair can do wonders for a comely GS-6.

These contrasts are not accidental; they are governed by the formal rules—both written and unwritten—that determine which symbols go with what status. The full flavor of the written codes can be savored only by verbatim quotation. This is from Admin. Serv. Cir. No. 33, Supp. 7; Revised March 7, 1957; Section 3: SPECIAL RESTRICTIONS—EXECUTIVE TYPE FURNITURE AND FURNISHINGS, which cautions:

A. *Limitations.* GSA Regulations 1-III-204.03 limits the use of executive furniture and furnishings to personnel in Grade GS-15 and above; and to chiefs of bureaus of other major organizational elements corresponding to the bureau level. The GSA in placing a limitation on the use of such items has established a minimum standard of use and has in no way authorized nor established criteria which are to be construed as entitling individuals at or above the prescribed levels to any or all of the items.

Translated, this means the official may have to haggle to get a complete set of symbols. The proper procedure for getting a more prestigious inkstand is then set forth:

C. *Statement of Compliance.* In support of the acquisition of executive type furniture and furnishings, the purchase or other acquisition files of the ordering activity shall state the proposed manner of acquisition and shall contain the following certification signed by the Property Accounting Officer or requisition approving officer as appropriate:

"This is to certify that the executive type furniture and/ or furnishings described above are to be acquired for the use of (Name of Person), (Grade), (Organizational Title), and that no similar or like items are being used by persons below the levels authorized in subsection 3A of Administrative Services Circular No. 33, Supplement No. 7."

Translated, this means that in order to preserve the proper status connotations, the applicant must promise that no undeserving underlings wind up with the wrong style of water carafe, or with waste baskets of an executive shape.

In practice, there is considerable variation from agency to agency in dividing the spoils of promotion. In the Federal Trade Commission, for example, the color of rug, type of swivel chair, and the shade of wood and leather tell a good deal to those in the know. According to informants, the top men at FTC—grades of GS-15 and over—are entitled to a royal broadloom carpet. There is a special rug which customarily goes to those who have the rating but not the status of a manager—a red broadloom. Others, below a GS-14 but of professional status, get a shaggy rust-colored rug of lesser quality. Field officers, who have a local status but not that of a higher-up at headquarters, get a green broadloom. So formalized is the system that when a new blue rug goes into an official's suite, no words are needed to announce that a new status (and the accompanying raise) has been achieved.

As to swivel chairs, subtle distinctions are noted between stenographic chairs (plastic, padded, no arms), plain wooden swivel chairs with no arms, armed wooden swivel chairs, plastic padded swivel chairs with wooden arms, leather swivel chairs with no arms, and so on. The men at the top, of course, preside from high-backed judge chairs. At the upper levels, the color of leather can be revealing; the top status seems to belong to the dark blue-green variety. It is also reported that the color of furniture becomes darker at the higher rungs—ascending from a bland maple and culminating in a rich mahogany.

In the State Department, everything from desk size, placement of telephone, and type of flag is charged with status meanings. The GS-15 automatically receives an executive desk that measures 66 x 40 inches—but at the rank of Assistant Secretary, the proportions increase to a more magisterial 72 x 48 inches. Telephones are telltale. Below a GS-15 rating, the telephone, naturally, sits on the desk. To the lowest status GS-15, goes a wooden telephone table costing about $40. The highest-rating GS-15 (a Director) is given a telephone cabinet, complete with drawers and doors, at a cost of about $70. As to flags, nobody under an Assistant Secretary can hang this prized emblem of office. The Assistant Secretaries get a 3 x 5 foot flag; the Under Secretaries move up to a 4½ x 5½ foot flag—and *the* Under Secretary gets a flag of office. Similar protocol governs draperies, coffee tables, club chairs, lamps, bookcases, and three-cushioned sofas.

To some of the younger GS-12s, whose manner is as caressingly bland as an Assistant Secretary's, it is cause for humiliation that their office decor proclaims their lowly station. Thus, when the State Department moved to new quarters in Foggy Bottom, a special status game was played by the junior executives. When the Superintendent of Moving was not around to watch, the younger men would slip into Old State and slip off with rugs, squared-off waste-baskets, and perhaps even an armchair or two. They then slipped their booty into the new building, where it was hidden until the Superintendent of Moving left the premises. Then out would come the rugs, the chairs, and the squared-off wastebaskets with their aura of inflated status. It is on private initiative like this that the safety of the free world rests.

Or used to rest. President Kennedy has already introduced some heretical new notions. "Let every public servant know," Mr. Kennedy said in his State of the Union Message, ". . . that a man's rank or reputation in this Administration will be determined by the size of the job he does, and not by the size of the staff, his office, or his budget." It remains to be seen if this spirit will be translated into the tribal rituals of government.

IV

For our final stop we return to Capitol Hill, and again seek the obscurer corners. This time, we follow a well-worn path to the lower level of the old House Office Building, where the recording studios are located. Within, we find two studios, one cunningly contrived to look like a Congressman's office—complete with desk, books, and a window-view of the Capitol Dome. This is the format most Congressmen prefer for the filmed programs they supply to local television stations.

The facilities are available at bargain rates. A member pays only for the film itself—$4.80 for eighty feet. Thus, a Congressman can prepare a five-minute program for as little as $16 to $20. The content can vary from a personal report, an interview, or a travelogue based on a foreign tour. If the member is a dullard, his party can be relied upon to provide advice.

During the Eisenhower Administration, the Republican Congressional Campaign Committee displayed special ingenuity in "exploiting" the new medium. Aides would prepare a list of questions for a Cabinet official. The Secretary would then sit in the studio for a separate recording of his "I'm-glad-you-asked-me-that" replies. Then, Republican Congressmen would file into the studio to put all their eloquence into the list of questions that the Secretary had answered a few days before. Technicians would blend the two tapes together to create a simulated interview—while the Congressmen, presumably, would rush to the House floor for a fiery denunciation of Charles Van Doren and television "frauds."

It is innovations like this that explain the remark of one of the ablest administrative assistants on Capitol Hill: "Once a member of Congress gets here, there is no excuse on earth for his ever being defeated." An incumbent always has a political advantage, but in recent years the advantage has become truly formidable. In addition to his salary, a Senator or a Representative receives special allowances for telegrams, toll calls, travel, stationery, stamps, and office staff (a Congressman can hire a $17,500 staff, while in the upper house the annual salary allowance rises to $28,740 for members from the biggest states). He can use—and abuse—subsidized facilities ranging from a postal frank to low-cost printing on Government presses.

Most members devote a large share of their resources on a day-in, day-out publicity campaign. Aside from mass mailings, the press release is the basic instrument for personal promotion. The handout has long been an institution; in the 1947 edition of the *Official Congressional Handbook* prepared for Capitol secretaries, great stress was placed on the importance of preparing and distributing news releases. With professional firmness, the *Handbook* instructed: "(1) State the facts; (2) Leave out the 'puffs'; (3) Keep it brief; (4) Measure news value."

But in recent years, the publicity battleground has shifted to television, and a whole arsenal of new weapons has been devised. History may yet record February 12, 1946 as one of the momentous days in the evolution of Congress. As part of a Lincoln Day ceremony, the first telecast was beamed from the Capitol. On January 3, 1947, a joint session of Congress was televised for the first time. Like the proverbial camel's nose, the TV camera was in the tent.

Soon, Congress established a recording studio, and the demand became so great that separate facilities were later established for each chamber. The Senate now uses six large rooms in the Capitol basement for recording purposes—and when the New Senate Office Building was erected, great care was taken to install roomy television facilities in the major hearing rooms (the House has remained fustily old-fashioned and still prohibits the televising of committee investigations).

Thus, the press release has been supplemented by the film clip—a visual blurb for the man in office. In his 1958 campaign for Governor, Nelson Rockefeller led the way by providing free film clips of his daily speeches to New York television stations. Since then, the more media-minded members of Congress have taken to preparing 30-second filmed interviews when their comments have news value for local stations at home.

The use of television is not always partisan and self-serving. Senator Philip A. Hart of Michigan has shown that the canned programs may be of genuine value. After his election in 1958, Mr. Hart prepared a series of thirteen interview programs of impressive range and thoughtfulness. Included in these 15-minute programs were lively discussions with Harry Truman on the value of primaries and with George V. Allen on the problems of the U.S. Information Agency. Senator Hart's resourceful administrative assistant, William Welsh, foresees a time when important Senatorial fact-finding committees will submit both a written and a filmed report. This could be of palpable value in informing the electorate on such varied problems as water resources and space exploration.

But the sceptics in Washington fear the Gresham's Law governing the publicity factory on Capitol Hill, *i.e.*, that the cheap and spurious may debase the worth of television originating in Congress. As in commercial television, for every *Omnibus* and *See It Now*, there will probably be a hundred political equivalents of *Gunsmoke*, *Our Gal Sunday*, and *This Is Your Life*. And the hapless challenger in Congressional elections may find himself running against Davy Crockett.

V

All of the things we have seen—the measured calligraphy of the Autopen, the rites of prestige, and the stratagems of the film clip—all of these are examples of the importance attached to the methodology of politics in Washington. It is not too harsh a judgment to say that this is the pervasive preoccupation of the Capital. Characteristically, when the question of national purpose became an "issue," the response of President Eisenhower was to appoint a Commission on National Goals, which has contributed still another report to the towering sheaf of ponderously unreadable committee documents. During the campaign, when national prestige became an "issue," the ultimate resort was to opinion polls concerning our "image" abroad. This dependence on polls and committees points to a fundamental *malaise* along the Potomac.

Washington has a single mistress—politics—and the city is a model of monogamous passion. This is what gives the Capital its peculiar and fascinating flavor. Joseph and Stewart Alsop, certified insiders, have this to say about the anatomy of conversation at even informal gatherings:

> Social conversation in Washington is almost invariably composed, in equal parts, of personal gossip, political dispute, and the eternal news of real estate, which fascinates Washingtonians because so many of the city's politicians and officials are only birds of passage, and are therefore always changing nests.
>
> Only the rare eccentrics, like Alice Roosevelt Longworth, can ever be induced to talk about books; and the arts, history, philosophy, and such-like subjects are best avoided, unless you want the reputation of an infernal bore.

Strenuous efforts are being made, to be sure, to seduce the city into an occasional infidelity. With technical cunning, the National Art Gallery has wired its rooms for sound so that visitors with portable head sets can hear tape-recorded lectures. But its openings are diplomatic events; only an eccentric Congressman will otherwise be found in its halls. A recently formed Institute of Contemporary Arts imports well-known writers and poets, who are greeted like alien potentates by the local press; but foundations subsidize this worthy effort.* A new Washington Opera Society performs four works a year; but Washington remains the only major world capital without an opera house (when the Metropolitan makes its biennial visit, it performs at the Loew's Capitol Theatre).

Thus it was wholly in character that when the Nobel Prize for Literature was awarded in 1960 to a Washington resident, scarcely anybody should have heard of him. Alexis Leger, the distinguished French poet who writes under the name of Saint-John Perse, had lived in Georgetown for twenty years; he could have lived in Timbuktu. A day after his award was announced, the Washington *Post* surveyed the city's bookstores and libraries and concluded that "you'd never guess that the winner . . . is a Washington resident." One bookshop proprietor confessed that he had never heard of the man, while others lacked a single volume by the Nobel Laureate.

Even the Beats have despaired of colonizing Washington. A brief, semi-comic attempt was made by a poet named William A. Walker (author of *A-w-w Hell*) to establish a coffee shop, but the police and zoning officials turned back the raffish invaders. James Truitt, a perceptive student of the Beat, wound up a local survey with almost an audible sigh: "You can't grow weeds or flowers (choose one) in a desert. Washington has no Bohemian and creative tradition, no cafe and music hall life. Like there's no air, Man."

---

* Perhaps to beguile the city, the Institute's 1960-61 program contains three events featuring the reassuring word "image": "The Image of Man Returns to Art" (Paul Tillich); "A Question of Image" (Martha Graham); and "Education and the Image of Man" (Max Lerner).

Scholars, artists, and philosophers; the men of finance and commerce; the elite of the theater and publishing—in sum, the people apart from politics who supply a context to events and keep government in its proper place, all these are for the most part missing from the stage in Washington.

The result is that Washington has, in effect, become a company town, and events are viewed almost exclusively in terms of their day-to-day effect on the dominant industry. This perspective distorts and disfigures the shape of events. For a week, the press is crowded with the current crisis—whether it is Sherman Adams, the Congo, or a mouse in space—and for a brief time all talk seems to center on the political implications of the current sensation. Then the headlines fade, and the cameras swerve to a new spectacular. It is as if the city were entranced by a brilliant shifting tableau with only the vaguest connecting plot. "Nothing has a drift or relation," in the words of Newman, "nothing has a history or a promise."

In any event, this was the prevailing condition during the Eisenhower years. A mood of change could be detected in the first months of the Kennedy Administration as the door of the White House was opened to poets and professors—and as the First Lady made clear her feeling that the language of life contained more than the prose of state. Indeed, as the next chapter suggests, cultural urbanity is one of the qualities that defines the heirs to the New Deal.

3 /

The Coming of the Smooth Deal

> The time to worry about this country is not when we are battling among ourselves, for it is then that our democracy functions best. The time to worry is when all is "moderation."
>
> —SAMUEL LUBELL

IF THE 1960 PRESIDENTIAL CAMPAIGN heralded a new theatrical approach to politics, the *dramatis personae* had already been established two years before. In the Congressional elections of that year, there was a wholesale turnover of the cast. Senators who had been fixtures in the troglodyte wing of the Republican Party bowed from the stage; *East Lynne* had played its last. Some, like Senator Jenner of Indiana and Senator Martin of Pennsylvania, retired without facing the voters. Others, like Senator Bricker of Ohio and Senator Revercomb of West Virginia, were defeated. The only survivor in 1958 was Senator Goldwater of Arizona, who has managed to clothe pre-Silurian ideas in a Brooks Brothers suit.

From courthouse to Congress, the voting in 1958 confirmed the emergence of a new collective personality in American politics, a personality—the word is peculiarly apt

—most readily apparent in the Democratic Party, but which peeked through among the Republicans as well. It is a personality which has produced a new style of liberal politics.

At the outset, it should be noted that our political vocabulary suffers from cultural lag. Surely it is misleading to describe the clean-shaven crop of Senators and Governors recently elected on the Democratic ticket as New or Fair Dealers. They are, to be sure, "liberals" in the sense of paying their fealty to Franklin Roosevelt, the TVA, and the Social Security Act. But New Dealers? Assuredly not. Harry Truman and Harold Ickes exemplify the New Deal personality in one familiar form; fiercely partisan, pungently outspoken, and pugnaciously self-righteous. Or there are Senators Humphrey and Douglas, two true-blue New Dealers who already seem a bit like relics from the past. In another variant, the phrase suggests the Brain Truster —the irrepressible innovator and impudent intellectual: Rexford Tugwell, Adolf A. Berle, Jerome Frank, and Thurman Arnold immediately come to mind.

A glance at the prudent liberals who now predominate in the Democratic Party suggests why this older association won't do and why a new term is sorely required. Pugnacity, more often than not, has given way to an earnest exurbanite sincerity; passion to a bland smile. And the Brain Truster has been shrunk to an academic egghead, content to hatch more modest schemes.

II

In a phrase, the New Deal has given way to the Smooth Deal, and I do not intend the term to be wholly pejorative. Certainly the older breed of liberals tended to crankiness, to oversimplification of issues, to hyper-partisanship, and even to occasional demagogy—Huey Long's "Every Man a King" nostrum was in some ways a caricature of New Deal thinking. If the Smooth Dealers seem drab by comparison, they also tend to be more fair-minded, better educated, less hysterical, more aware of the limitations of political reform, and more culturally sophisticated. In 1958, one observer remarked that if either Mr. Kennedy or Mr. Rockefeller should become tenants in the White House, at least the quality of the paintings would improve.

The reference to Mr. Rockefeller as a Smooth Dealer was deliberate; one trait of the new liberal is his marked lack of old-style partisanship—indeed, without a party label it might be impossible to tell the men in the middle apart. Surely it is one of the ironies of the 1958 election that while President Eisenhower was inveighing against the menace of "radicalism," in most major Senate races the Democratic candidate was closer to the Modern Republican ideal than his rusting Old Guard opponent. Many of the Smooth Dealers, in fact, seem perfectly interchangeable, like parts in a 1960 Chevrolet Suburban; it is altogether conceivable that Republican Senators Javits, Cooper, and Clifford Case could run as liberal Democrats, while Senators Symington and Harrison Williams could be Republicans whom the New York *Herald Tribune* would beamingly endorse.

This change in tempo and mood was observable throughout the country, but of all the many elections perhaps none was more revealing than the mealtime marathon conducted in New York between Averell Harriman and Nelson Rockefeller. In many ways, former Governor Harriman was the orthodox New Dealer unable to learn the new rhythm of politics. Like an Old Roman, he was unable to repackage his wood-crate personality in a more contemporary plastic box. Despite the best coaches, Harriman could not mask his essential inner-directed gruffness with a smile. As a result, Mr. Rockefeller outcharmed his halting rival and made impressive inroads on the traditional liberal-labor vote—especially among the women. What was perhaps the most interesting document in the campaign was a column in the New York *Post* in which one of Mr. Rockefeller's converts explained why at the last moment the house organ of Manhattan liberalism pleaded with its readers not to vote for Mr. Harriman. Mrs. Dorothy Schiff, the *Post's* publisher, confided in her "Dear Reader" column:

> It was obvious to those who knew Nelson Rockefeller that he was always a considerate, sincere, warm, very human being. In contrast, people who had worked with Averell Harriman had often been dismayed by the difficult personality traits displayed by him.

The key phrase is "difficult personality traits." In this Age of the Image, it is fatal for a candidate to flunk his Rorschach test.

I I I

A few questions are in order. How did the Smooth Deal get its start? Why did it find such a receptive audience? And what changes does it involve in the flavor of American politics?

In some ways, the key figure in the 1958 election was a man who was not a candidate at all, nor an office-holder, and who indeed was only marginally involved in the campaign. Yet Adlai Stevenson, despite being a two-time loser for the Presidency, had a more pervasive effect on the tone and quality of the campaign than the General in the White House, who loosed an occasional thunderbolt, or the Vice President, who wielded the more lethal cutlery. This is because Mr. Stevenson is both an agent and a symbol of the change in liberal politics, and the election was unquestionably a victory for that moderate brand of liberalism which Mr. Stevenson exemplifies. Closer in conviction, manner, and temperament to Nelson Rockefeller than to Harry Truman, Adlai Stevenson is the example par excellence of the patrician turned politician. Ivy-educated (Princeton, '22), he speaks in the accents of genteel liberalism, and his appeal is strongest to that growing middlebrow-plus group that has cut its teeth on the New Deal, makes knowing cracks about the political slant in *Time,* and furnishes the audience for such diverse phenomena as *Peanuts,* good music stations, and Mort Sahl.

To this group, tired of the banalities of the Republican Party, and too sophisticated to swallow whole the slogans of the New Deal, the personality of Adlai Stevenson has served as a tonic and lure. During the Governor's two campaigns for the Presidency, Volunteers for Stevenson flourished with special *éclat* in the middlebrow enclaves of the suburbs. On college campuses across the country, if you saw a foreign car it invariably sported a Stevenson sticker; the Cadillacs liked Ike.

The end result was an influx of new talent, new candidates, and new leadership in the Democratic Party—indeed, one began to hear about "Stevenson-type" Democrats and even "Adlites." Thus, in one of those recurrent ironies of American politics, Stevenson, though twice the loser, presided over a reinvigoration of his party—while the winner, even from the exalted heights of the White House, proved impotent in his task of "modernizing" the Grand

Old Party. Despite the best efforts of Robert Montgomery and Henry Luce, the party that boasted the support of Madison Avenue was unable in eight years to rid itself of the musty McKinley odor. It was symptomatic that two of the Republican Party's most promising new personalities —Governors Rockefeller and Hatfield (of Oregon)—owed their victory in 1958 in good part to the fact that they avoided identification with their party and its national administration.

I V

This plastic surgery under the auspices of the losing candidate has its precedents; three instances are especially notable. There is the case of William Jennings Bryan, three times the Democratic Presidential candidate, three times defeated—and yet successful in restoring to his party something of the radical flavor it had during the Age of Jackson. Before Bryan swept the 1896 Democratic convention with his "Cross of Gold" speech, the party had virtually been held in tithe by the Eastern banks under the brokership of Grover Cleveland. After Bryan had joined hands with the Populists in a crusade against the "Goldbugs," the party lost its preferred stock aura and was seldom again regarded as entirely "safe" by the paladins of high finance. Often wrong-headed, pompous, superficial, and plain silly, Bryan had nonetheless breathed back into the party its reforming sense of mission. Richard Hofstadter, who is no admirer of Bryan, concedes this much: "The Commoner, always defeated, had, in the course of a sixteen-year quest for issues, effectively turned public attention upon one reform after another; and many of his proposals had a core of value." Both figuratively and literally (by his votes at the 1912 convention), Bryan made possible the election of Woodrow Wilson, prophet of the New Freedom.

But the Democratic Party remained essentially an agrarian party with only transient urban ties until another great loser, Al Smith, broadened its base and turned a minority party into a majority coalition which still holds sway. Samuel Lubell, who first noted its significance, called the 1928 Presidential election the "Smith Revolution," because for the first time the country's biggest cities, with their Catholic-Jewish-immigrant electorate, were carried into the Democratic column. For the most part, the cities have remained there since.

It was this urban-agrarian coalition that Franklin Roosevelt fused so successfully through four Presidential campaigns, and which prevailed until two other losing candidates—Wendell Willkie and Thomas E. Dewey—found ways of channeling new energy into a moribund Republican Party. Indeed, Willkie's prairie-fire nomination campaign in 1940 was reminiscent of Bryan's siege of Chicago in 1896. Willkie, an unknown armed mainly with a chant ("We Want Willkie"), became the catalyst for party reform, while Dewey, possessing the more persuasive leverage of New York's electoral votes, became the executant. Between them, Willkie and Dewey attracted homeless moderates to the Republican cause, and made it respectable for an intelligent person to confess sympathy with a conservative party. Finally, in 1952, the internationalist and moderately progressive wing of the party rode to power on the coat-tails of a hero whose pre-eminent virtue was that he had a likable smile and was not associated with the party he was called on to lead.

But this insulation from politics, this above-the-battle prose which so strengthened Mr. Eisenhower as a candidate, proved a disaster for his party. The election of the General signaled a retreat from politics at precisely the moment when the Republican Party could best be purged from within. As a result, the reformation begun by Willkie and Dewey remained unfinished, and the various crabbed rightists who give Republicanism such a sour tone remained unmolested, unrepentant, unfumigated. Symbolically, the major public monument built during the Eisenhower years was a memorial tower to Robert A. Taft.

V

It was within this vacuum created by President Eisenhower's ineptness or inertia that the Stevenson Revolution has taken place. Surely it is a remarkable tribute to the Democratic Party as an institution that even in its worst defeats it has found the seeds of regeneration. In retrospect, one can see that even in the midst of the 1952 disaster, the beginnings of change were evident. There was the victory of Senator John Kennedy in Massachusetts, following a cultivated tea-party campaign; and there was the fact that Stevenson carried Philadelphia where a reform Democratic administration had taken office a year before. In Senator Kennedy and Philadelphia's Mayor (and subsequently Senator) Joseph S. Clark, the new liberalism found its two most attractive advance agents.

Mr. Clark and Mr. Kennedy were pre-eminently tacticians of the soft sell. Suavely tailored and unabashedly good-looking, both spoke in the urbane accents of a middlebrow-plus, and could contribute a literate article to the *Atlantic* without much ghostly assistance. Both came from a background of ease and comfort, both attended Harvard, and both brought to politics an attitude of *pro bono publico,* a clean-cut sincerity, and a modulated commitment to the tenets of the Liberal Enlightenment. Both men were equally at home at a Fairfield County barbecue—unlikely torch-bearers indeed for a party damned as "radical" by President Eisenhower.

The years since 1952 have seen a steady increase in the ranks of liberal leaders cast in the Stevenson-Kennedy-Clark mold. In 1953, Governor Robert Meyner took control of New Jersey's state house and gave consanguine links to the movement by marrying a relative of Adlai Stevenson. Although a Republican Smooth Dealer, Clifford Case, won New Jersey's senatorial race in 1954, Mr. Meyner rounded out his victory by helping to elect the youthful Harrison Williams to the Senate in 1958.

Meanwhile, in California, the Democratic Party was rejuvenated by a club movement led by Stevensonian Democrats. Aided by Republican blunders, the Stevenson wing carried the state in 1958, electing Edmund (Pat) Brown as Governor, Clair Engle as Senator, and winning control of the legislature. Further northward, in Oregon, another Stevenson Democrat—perhaps too ebullient to be regarded as a Smooth Dealer—was able to add Senator to his frequent byline in *Harper's*. But if there were doubts about the late Richard L. Neuberger, there could be none about Senator Henry (Scoop) Jackson of Washington. In Idaho, a state where the class war used to be more than a slogan, the miners installed boyish Frank Church in the Senate, where he became at age 32 the youngest of the Smooth.

In Michigan, former Governor G. Mennen Williams, a throwback to the New Deal whose trade-mark is a bow tie, created a private empire beginning with his 1948 election. However, the state's Junior Senator, Philip A.

Hart, shows more urbane inclinations. In 1958 and 1960, Michigan Republicans adopted the tactics of their brethren in New York and Oregon by putting up their own Smooth Dealer as the candidate to end Democratic control of the state. Their choice was Paul Bagwell, a professor of speech at Michigan State University, who annoyed party regulars by his liberalism and intellectual tendencies, and who ran a vigorous, if losing, race. "Something resembling a Stevensonian cult has formed around Bagwell," reported *Time* magazine.

Minnesota, where the old Farmer-Labor tradition still has a lingering hold, is associated with Senator Hubert H. Humphrey, a politician too bumptious to qualify as Smooth. But the state has also sent to the Senate Eugene McCarthy, as polished an egghead as will likely ever grace those chambers. Because of his brilliant nominating speech at Los Angeles, Mr. McCarthy was clearly the idol of the Stevensonians at the Democratic Convention.

The mention of McCarthy recalls Wisconsin, and that unpredictable state also went Smooth. Surely few elections contain as many paradoxes as the special vote held in August, 1957, to fill the vacancy left on the death of Senator Joseph McCarthy. Not only did the voters fill his seat with a member of the "party of treason," but they also chose a candidate with degrees from *both* Yale ('38) and Harvard (M.B.A., M.P.A.), who was a former associate in J. P. Morgan's firm, and who had been wed to a Rockefeller. It was a tribute to the appeal of Senator William Proxmire, since re-elected, whose youthfully engaging manner contrasted so strikingly with the belch-and-bearhug traits of Joe McCarthy. As Governor, the voters chose the personable and handsome Gaylord Nelson.

Then there is the case of Maine. In 1954, the voters in

this most venerably Republican state elected their third
Democratic Governor since the Civil War, later re-elected
him, and in 1958 sent Edmund S. Muskie to the Senate.
The most Lincolnesque of the Smooth, Mr. Muskie is one
of the ablest and most likable figures in the Stevenson wing
of the party. Characteristically, the Maine Democratic
Party was revitalized by a close-knit group of Stevensonian
liberals, led by State Chairman John C. Donovan, a professor of government at Bates College, and former Congressman Frank Coffin. In a detailed study of Mr. Coffin's
1956 campaign, Professor Donovan concluded that the
Congressman's victory "may be ascribed to a new sort of
politics—a politics of youth, of amateurs, substantially
without patronage or corruption."

VI

Decidedly, there *is* a new sort of politics prevailing in
more and more states. If the day of the impassioned New
Dealer has passed, the era of the hack and the ward-heeler
as a candidate is also vanishing. Whatever else can be said
of the new liberals, they are neither uninspired nor illiterate, and for this trend to a more enlightened approach to
politics much of the credit belongs to Adlai Stevenson. It
was fitting that among the freshmen Congressmen elected
in 1958 (and re-elected in 1960) were two candidates who
shared the distinction of serving successively on Mr. Stevenson's 1956 campaign staff in the same post: Ken Hechler
of West Virginia and John Brademas of Indiana. Both
headed the research division for Mr. Stevenson in a campaign that was a lost cause only in a narrow, immediate
sense.

Writing in 1960, Arthur M. Schlesinger, Jr., rightly observed:

> The Democratic Party underwent a transformation in its years in the wilderness. To a considerable degree that transformation was the work of a single man—Adlai Stevenson. In his eight years as titular leader, Stevenson renewed the Democratic Party. . . .
>
> Though his supporters failed to get him the nomination, historians may well regard Stevenson as the true victor in the convention. He had remade the Democratic Party, and largely in his own image, even if he was not himself to be the beneficiary. More perhaps than either of them fully realizes, Kennedy today is the heir and executor of the Stevenson revolution.

Immediately after the Los Angeles convention, it was apparent that Mr. Kennedy was adding his own variations to the new liberal image. In the Democratic primary in Rhode Island a political novice won the Senate nomination by upsetting a former Governor and a former U.S. Attorney General. He was Claiborne Pell, a handsome Princetonian who became the candidate to succeed Theodore Francis Green, the oldest Senator (age 93) ever to hold office. The Associated Press reported: "Pell, a 41-year-old Newport socialite and businessman who has a home in Georgetown, sought during the hard-fought primary campaign to link his youth with that of 43-year-old Senator John F. Kennedy, the Democratic presidential nominee."

In Mr. Kennedy's home state, the same phenomenon occurred. Billing himself as "Springfield's Great Young Mayor," 35-year-old Tom O'Connor defeated the incumbent Governor of Massachusetts in the Democratic senatorial primary. (Mr. Kennedy, too, was 35 when he first ran for the Senate.) The format was familiar in the campaign that followed; the crew-cut young Mayor whirled through the state attending a daily round of "Teas for Tom." But Lipton was not enough; Massachusetts perversely re-elected Senator Leverett Saltonstall.

VII

The 1958 elections, then, confirmed the emergence of a novel kind of American politician—the candidate as a confident amateur, who, though he may work in tandem with the Old Pro, strives above all to look more like a Suburban Everyman than a politician. He is a candidate who despite a background of wealth is capable of the relaxed and homely touch: interestingly, Mr. Stevenson's hole-in-the-shoe became a campaign emblem, while Mr. Rockefeller wore a leather patch on his jacket virtually as a panache. He is not afraid to confess that he has once read (or written) a book.

Thus, in the framework of liberal politics, the country is entering an era in which breeding, intelligence, and the absence of "difficult personality traits" will be every bit as important as the advocacy of ideas. The trend to the Smooth is understandable, given the changing circumstances of American life. There is the obvious influence of the television cameras, which turn an exposing lens on every psychic wrinkle a candidate may possess. The extraordinary increase in college attendance has created a climate favorable for a candidate who admits that he once went to school. The tidal migrations from city to suburb and thence to exurb have wrought a change in mores in which the word "togetherness" has a wholesome rather than repugnant ring.

And the new style reflects the influence of the super-market's well-known packaging techniques.

At its best, the new liberalism can produce spokesmen of eloquence, insight, and energy. In his campaign speeches of 1952, Adlai Stevenson reached heights rarely achieved in public statements. His candor, his stress on the complexity of events, his wit, and his respect for reason made Mr. Stevenson's speeches an enduring contribution to political literature. Governor Rockefeller, too, has shown a sobriety and dedication rare among popular politicians. And Mr. Kennedy displays an incisiveness, a sophistication about ideas, and a talent for command that belies his old reputation of being merely Smooth.

But at his lowest level, the Smooth Dealer is too obsessed by the problems of his "image" to explore the controversial issues of his time; he is too impressed by opinion polls, and lacking in interior conviction; he is too prone to conceive of electoral survival as an end in itself; his nose is so implanted in the middle-of-the-road that his eyes lose sight of the horizon. No one has been more critical of this pervasive blandness than Adlai Stevenson himself. "The style of our age reinforces a quiescent mood," Mr. Stevenson declared in 1960. "It is a style framed by consumption and designed to increase it. Clearly if you want to sell something, you don't first make the customer mad at you."

In short, the gain in manners among the new liberals has at times been overbalanced by a melancholy loss in gumption. Such indeed was the case in the 86th Congress, reputedly the most liberal since the days of Franklin Delano Roosevelt.

4 /

Suitors in the Cloakroom

> There are periods when the principles of experience
> need to be modified, when hope and trust and instinct
> claim a share with prudence in the guidance of affairs,
> when, in truth, *to dare* is the highest wisdom.
>
> —WILLIAM ELLERY CHANNING

YEARS AGO, WHEN JOHN F. KENNEDY was a stripling Congressman from Massachusetts, he incautiously observed: "The House is run by a crowd of old men who would have been pensioned off years ago if they were in private industry." The diagnosis is more apt than ever; the sleepy pace of age tranquilizes both chambers of Congress. In recent sessions, the mood of weary surrender has even afflicted most of the younger members who once lent a crackle of excitement to the *Congressional Record*.

Muckrakers used to belabor Congress for its failings off the floor, where lobbyists used their influence for dubious ends. The lobbyists are still at work, but the shame of Congress now is what takes place on the floor, in full view of the public. Most often, nothing really takes place.

Writing in 1879, Woodrow Wilson contended that *"debate* is the essential function of a popular representative body. In the severe, distinct, and sharp enunciation of underlying principles, the unsparing examination and telling criticism of opposite positions . . . we see the best, the only effective means of educating public opinion."

Compare this with the theory of leadership held by Lyndon Johnson, as described by columnist Marquis Childs:

> Public controversy is bad—bad for the party and bad for the country. This is the heart of the Johnson conviction. You have got to work things out in the cloakroom and then when you've got them worked out, you can debate a little before. In the politics of manipulation and maneuver, Johnson has proved once again he is a master. But this ignores the content, the substance, of political give and take. It draws off the fight, the conviction, the zeal.

During the 86th Congress, the new liberals by and large accepted the Johnson approach, with its attendant implications: desultory debate, lack of roll calls, and backstage bargaining rather than public controversy. Midway in the session, Douglass Cater of *The Reporter* magazine described the result; he noted that Congress, despite its large Democratic majority, "had failed to create a sense of urgency to serve as a counterbalance to the lack of urgency displayed by the Eisenhower Administration. The Democrats have simply not demonstrated, except in isolated and sometimes irrelevant instances, any basic disagreement with the President's program."

This failure of the liberal majority in Congress to challenge the conservative mood and create a new set of legislative priorities now clouds the prospects for President Kennedy's dealing with an even less liberal Congress.

I I

"This isn't a session of Congress," snapped an imperti-
nent New Yorker, "this is a kissing bee." The year was
1931, and the remark was directed to Speaker John Nance
Garner by Fiorello LaGuardia, then a Republican Congressman and all-purpose irritant. History has come full
circle, and a Texan is again Speaker of the House, while
another Texan (like Mr. Garner) has risen to the Vice
Presidency of the United States. But there has been no
voice like LaGuardia's on Capitol Hill.

LaGuardia's service as Mayor of New York City has
obscured his bouncy role in the House of Representatives
during the 1920's. Time and again during the Coolidge
and Hoover era, LaGuardia led insurgent forays against
the leadership of both major parties. When Hoover's
Secretary of the Treasury, Andrew Mellon, proposed a
new tax law which favored the rich, it was easy to win
the support of Democrat Garner. But not of LaGuardia,
who guided a successful floor revolt against the Mellon bill. "All was serene a few days ago," complained
The New York Times, ". . . Then Mr. LaGuardia tossed
a nice, new shiny monkey wrench." Sputtered a Midwest newspaper, "Chaos reigns in Congress . . . the
blatant and irresponsible members of Congress, led by
such men as LaGuardia of New York, a product of the
steerage and Ellis Island of a few years back, have dipped
their fingers in the gore of confiscation and gone on an
orgy which they themselves call 'soak the rich.' "

The rhetoric was typical of the times. During the most
complacent years of the 1920's, there was insistent dissent
on the floor of Congress. Midwest insurgents, who were

dubbed Sons of the Wild Jackass, fought for a whole range of reforms. Senator George Norris of Nebraska kept the demand alive for a Tennessee Valley Authority, while liberal Democrats like Senator Robert F. Wagner of New York and Progressives like Senator Robert M. La Follette, Jr., of Wisconsin repeatedly urged new welfare legislation. LaGuardia himself called for a national unemployment compensation system two years before Franklin Roosevelt came to Washington.

Most of the battles were lost. But when FDR was inaugurated in 1933, the ground had been prepared for the New Deal. The forum of Congress had been used to create a demand for new proposals, to draw up the agenda for Mr. Roosevelt. Thus the liberals of the 1920's effectively discharged their responsibility as minority spokesmen; with a few notable exceptions, their counterparts in the 1950's didn't even try. The 86th Congress, reputedly the most liberal since the high tide of the New Deal, produced little legislation and less excitement. With the exception of civil rights, the boldest proposals were warmed-over New Deal. On the whole, the Congressional liberals were reluctant to join controversy on such post-New Deal problems as the Cold War, the price and wage structure of a centralized private economy, and the cultural quality of American life (more specifically: television).

In private, liberal Democrats frequently deplored the languor on the Hill, and tended to lay the blame on three factors: (1) the lack of militancy of the Texas leadership; (2) the inertia in the White House; and (3) the complacent national mood. Still, all three conditions prevailed in the 1920's, and somehow the dissidents made themselves heard. It seems especially disingenuous to blame Lyndon B. Johnson for the liberal failure of nerve. Mr. Johnson was an official party leader and, like his predecessors, sought to apply the salve of compromise to party disputes. It was not Mr. Johnson's fault that the would-be insurgents failed to perform their role as effectively as the Texan did his.

III

Let us examine three areas where the paucity of real conflict was an especially grievous loss. The first involves Congress as a working organization, the second concerns foreign policy, and the final area touches on the vital matter of civil liberties.

It is an old story that Congress is ruled by its committees. The eighty-year-old diagnosis cf Woodrow Wilson still rings true:

> Power is nowhere concentrated; it is rather deliberately and of set policy scattered amongst many small chiefs. . . . These petty barons, some of them not a little powerful, but none of them within the reach of the full powers of rule, may at will exercise an almost despotic sway within their own shires, and sometimes threaten to convulse even the realm itself. . . .

Of all the moated fortresses, none has been more carefully guarded than the Rules Committee of the House, which in the last Congress was dominated by men who seemed to believe that feudalism was dangerously progressive. Yet this Committee must pass on all except appropriation bills, and can kill legislation or restrict the terms of its consideration on the floor. The chairman of Rules was and is a 76-year-old Virginian, Howard W. Smith, a courtly lieutenant of Senator Harry F. Byrd, who cheerfully admits: "I use every weapon I've got. That's why I'm here."

Over the years, the obstructionism of the Rules Committee has grown increasingly intolerable to liberal Democrats, and in 1959 there was brave talk about a revolt. The 86th Congress was about to convene, and the liberal representation was at the highest point in a generation. It seemed that a showdown was finally at hand.

A delegation of restive Democrats marched on Sam Rayburn's office, and the press watched expectantly for signs of a fight. But the Speaker permitted only the leader of the delegation, Chet Holifield of California, into his inner chamber; the rest cooled their heels outside. Soon, Mr. Holifield emerged and said that Mr. Rayburn had promised that from now on the Rules Committee would behave. Thus expired the revolt; the Speaker never bothered to make a statement of his own, and no floor fight was made on the procedural reforms sought by the rebels.

Anastas Mikoyan, the Soviet First Deputy Premier, happened to be a visitor in Washington, and this coincidence prompted a taunt from I. F. Stone, the editor of a peppery leftist newsletter:

> We're glad Mikoyan saw the Jefferson chandelier and the Dolly Madison mirror in Nixon's office, but we're sorry he missed other sights on Capitol Hill which would have taken the strangeness from the scene and made our visitor feel right at home. An example was the revolt of the liberal Democrats . . . which Speaker Rayburn put down with an efficiency Mikoyan might not have believed possible in our looser form of government.

Not many months later, *pace* Mr. Rayburn, the Rules Committee showed that it was not housebroken at all.

Senators Kennedy and Johnson arrived from the Los Angeles Convention to lead a special rump session of Congress; the pressure was intense to pass at least some of the legislation pledged in the Democratic platform. And the prestige of the Texas leadership was at stake. But Chairman Smith balked, blocked, and bargained; his party was unable to get anything substantial through. "This isn't Kennedy's Congress," fumed one Democrat. "It's Judge Smith's Congress."

It was at this point that the value of an earlier floor fight could be seen. Even if the revolt had failed, the groundwork for reform would have been laid by alerting the public to the hidden strings of power controlled by Mr. Smith. As it was, President Kennedy had to face, in his first days, the identical problem of minority rule within Congress. Only after a bitter siege, involving strenuous White House pressure and some possible compromise of his legislative program, did Mr. Kennedy secure a modest reform by the narrowest of margins.

Nor is it clear that the President's success is permanent; Chairman Smith pointedly assigned the three new members of his enlarged committee uncomfortable, hard-backed chairs, assuring them that they would not be serving very long. Subsequently, Mr. Smith relented—but only to the extent of providing softer chairs.

IV

The relationship of Congress to foreign policy is necessarily a delicate matter. Legislative meddling into the constitutional prerogatives of the Executive has often had mischievous results. Nonetheless, Congress does have an important constructive role in reviewing Administration policy. By the way it conditions public opinion, Congress in the long run can determine the President's range of choice.

A good example is the need, since the death of Stalin, to reformulate the premises of the Cold War. There have been radical changes in the political temper of Africa, Asia, and Latin America since Dean Acheson was Secretary of State. Missile technology has advanced to the point where the strategic worth of overseas bases needs re-examination. The rise of China, the ferment in Eastern Europe, the enlargement of the nuclear club—these are all new elements in the equation. Policies which might have been wholly valid in 1950—or even in 1956—might require more critical scrutiny in the 1960's.

Yet on the whole, even the more articulate members of Congress have failed to use their tongues in a way that might prepare opinion for policy changes. Instead, the tendency has been to cling to official homilies, to calcify rather than question prevailing dogmas. In extenuation, it can be argued that the abler members of Congress have had to fight a defensive battle against retrenchment. Nevertheless, the silence on the Hill has allowed an alarming gap to widen between the new power realities of the world and the way the American public sees those realities.

The most familiar example is the case of Red China. In the privacy of their offices, influential members of Congress deplore the rigidity of existing policy and speak hopefully of face-saving formulas which will enable the country to accept the inevitable—the admission of Peking into the United Nations. But on the floor of Congress, the Chinese mainland remains terra incognita. With a few rare exceptions—including Senator Clair Engle of California—members have refused to question the myths of

Far Eastern policy, to venture where at least Engle has dared to tread.

Less familiar, however, has been the failure of Congress to deal in an educative way about Latin America. Indeed, the reverse is true; recent debates have seemed to hark back to the days of Teddy Roosevelt's Big Stick. Discussions of Cuba have often become contests in denunciation, in which there has been little effort at illuminating the conditions which produce a Fidel Castro. During the debates on sugar legislation in 1960, leaders of both parties were so careful to avoid being soft on Castro that in the end the Dominican Republic wound up with a windfall slice of the Cuban sugar quota. It didn't seem to matter that this country, in concert with its neighbors, had broken relations with the Dominican dictatorship of Rafael Trujillo, whose regime was as unpopular in Latin America as Castro was on Capitol Hill.

It was at this time that Senator Allen J. Ellender of Louisiana helpfully commented, "I wish there was a Trujillo in every country of Latin America tonight." Whenever a member of Congress praises a Latin American *caudillo*, it is a front-page item elsewhere in the hemisphere, and our embassies must work overtime to explain the eccentricities of our politicians. On this occasion, as usual, not a single dissenting Senator rose to make clear that the voice of Ellender was not the voice of America.

Indeed, attacks on tyranny are too often directed exclusively at the Communist bloc. In July, 1959, Congress observed Captive Nations Week with a stern and no doubt deserved denunciation of dictatorship. But at the same time, Generalissimo Franco commemorated the 23rd anniversary of the Spanish Civil War, and the extinction of freedom suddenly became respectable. Among those who warmly congratulated Franco was Congressman Roland V. Libonatti of Illinois, who saluted Spain's contribution to the "common cause of liberty-loving nations" and begged forgiveness for "the outrageous acts committed against her [Spain] and the lack of support to her up to 1953." Only one member, Henry Reuss of Wisconsin, troubled to add as a mild afterthought that a liberalization of the Spanish tyranny might also be welcome.

Excessive zeal in attacking certain dictators can be a liability. Former Congressman Charles O. Porter of Oregon became something of a hero in Latin America because of his repeated attacks on the Trujillo regime (one of Porter's constituents, Gerald Lester Murphy, was found dead under strange circumstances in a Dominican jail; it is believed that Murphy was silenced for his role in the disappearance of Dr. Jesus de Galindez, a Trujillo critic who vanished from the streets of New York). But Trujillo has his friends in Congress. When Mr. Porter returned for his second term in 1959, he was kept in the obscurity of the Post Office and Civil Service Committee, where his indignation might focus on safer topics like second and third class mail.

In the Senate, several members have made notable contributions to foreign policy debates; Senator Mansfield has delivered thoughtful speeches on Africa and Latin America, Senator Humphrey has become a specialist in disarmament, and Senator Fulbright has presented adult views on European disengagement. But curiously, the most systematic attempt to define an alternative foreign policy was made not in the Senate but by a group of freshmen in the House.

This was the Liberal Project, founded and led by Robert Kastenmeier, the first Wisconsin Democrat in a quarter century to win the House seat once held by Robert M. La Follette, Sr. Ten Democratic Congressmen—seven of them freshmen—joined with Mr. Kastenmeier in an organized attempt to go beyond the platitudes of liberalism, especially in the area of foreign affairs. The average age of the freshmen was 39 years, and all except one had been elected in 1958 by margins of less than 55 per cent. In the circumstances, caution would have been expected; none of the freshmen had the luxury of a six-year Senate term.

Nevertheless, members of the group persistently raised questions on the floor and refused automatically to assume that the leadership knew best. At a series of evening seminars held at the home of Mrs. Harold Ickes, the Congressmen ignored tradition by consorting with intellectuals and discussing ideas (not "issues"). In May, 1960, the Project issued a 44-page statement highly critical of prevailing attitudes on foreign policy. The paper, which roughly embodied the ideas made familiar by Walter Lippmann and George Kennan, was prepared by James P. Warburg, a foreign policy analyst. The ideas themselves were not new; what was new was the fact that eleven Congressmen were bold enough to announce their agreement with the general approach, if not the details, of Mr. Warburg's statement.

All controversy represents a risk for a politician, and the freshmen were aware that their position might complicate their re-election prospects in marginal districts. In 1960, four of the freshmen won, and four were defeated along with a score of other Democrats. But win or lose, the young insurgents had the satisfaction of being more than ciphers on a voting machine.

V

If Congress sometimes seemed deaf to revolutionary sentiments abroad, it fully compensated by its oversensitiveness to revolutionary sects at home. Strangely, while Congressional debates reflected little awareness of the instability of the old order in Latin America, an observer might conclude that the United States itself was on the verge of being seized by a handful of Communists.

In both the House and Senate, special committees worked overtime hunting down fewer and fewer. Indeed, the smaller the Communist Party, the more terrible became the warnings of imminent peril from Congressman Francis E. Walter, chairman of the Committee on Un-American Activities. FBI Director J. Edgar Hoover, at appropriations time, also invariably managed to make this year's threat more ominous than last year's—despite a shrinkage in party rolls. Doubtless in the years ahead, when the party has dwindled to 123 members (exclusive of FBI men in disguise), four more Congressional committees will be needed to keep America alert. And when there are none left at all, perhaps Mr. Khrushchev will rent out a few to Chairman Walter so that the Committee can continue to justify its annual tribute of $327,000 or more.

During the 86th Congress, the House Committee made the most of a poor script. It looked into subversion in music schools, helped to stimulate a riot in San Francisco, hunted heretics in Puerto Rico (supposedly a semi-autonomous commonwealth), and found time to produce a movie which implied that only Communists favored its abolition. The Committee, however, did not scorn the amenities; a search through expense account records showed that the investigators charged the public for refreshments at the Persian Room, where presumably they were poring over the works of Lenin. It also developed that Richard Arens, the Committee's staff director, was serving as a paid consultant to an eccentric New York millionaire who was chiefly interested in proving the genetic inferiority of Negroes. Mr. Arens also turned up in Des Moines to warn a public meeting that Mr. Eisenhower's patriotism was in doubt because the President had introduced his grandchildren to Mr. Khrushchev. The Des Moines *Register* commented that Mr. Arens' "astounding speech . . . reinforced our belief that this Committee, which is now headed by Rep. Francis E. Walter, should be abolished."

But in the 86th Congress, so stocked with fiery liberals, only one member dared to demand abolition. On the several occasions that Congressman James Roosevelt of California spoke out against the Committee on the floor, not a single voice came to his support. Leaders of the House slipped the Committee appropriation through when Mr. Roosevelt was not around, to assure that there would be no dissent. The only reform was the removal of the ineffable Mr. Arens; he was promoted to a $19,000-a-year job as Commissioner of the United States Court of Claims.

In the Senate, the field was dominated by the Internal Security Subcommittee, headed by Democrats Thomas J. Dodd of Connecticut and James O. Eastland of Mississippi. These intrepid investigators found that the disloyalists in the State Department were back to their old game of giving countries to the Communists. As Messrs. Dodd and Eastland put it, "Cuba was handed to Castro and the Communists by a combination of Americans in the same way China was handed to the Communists." This judgment was based largely on the testimony of such expert witnesses as former Batista army officers and two former U.S. ambassadors to Cuba, Earl E. T. Smith and Arthur Gardner, both disgruntled amateurs known for their friendliness to the Batista regime. No attempt was made to hear the State Department's side. The Subcommittee also created a dubious precedent when it placed a British journalist, Kenneth Tynan, on the stand to explain his endorsement of a statement sympathetic to Castro.

But the liberal Democrats in the Senate, who speak indignantly about McCarthyism past, remained silent when these fellow members of the party of Thomas Jefferson dipped into McCarthy's briefcase of tricks. The Democratic leadership also gave no public sign of displeasure. Indeed, after the election when a vacancy developed on the Foreign Relations Committee, Senator Dodd was rewarded with the seat. He was chosen in preference to Senator Joseph S. Clark of Pennsylvania, even though by the rules of seniority Mr. Dodd's claim was weaker. Senator Dodd only assailed the State Department; Senator Clark, on occasion, criticized his party's leadership. In the morality of Capitol Hill, could this be the difference between venial and mortal sin?

5 /

Texas Leaves Its Landmarks

> The Senators themselves, once the teachers of morality
> and religion, now vow a thousand pounds of gold
> to decorate the Capitoline, gilding even Jupiter himself
> with cash, so that no one need be ashamed of his greed.
> —PETRONIUS, *Satyricon*, ca. A.D. 66

CONSERVATISM IN CONGRESS does not extend to all public problems; there is at least one area in which our national legislature displays a damn-the-tradition, spend-and-spend exuberance. This concerns the physical surroundings of Congress. "I found Rome built of sun-dried brick," boasted the Emperor Augustus, "I leave her clothed in marble." And perhaps not since the days of Augustus have the marble vendors been so busy as under the Texas proconsulate now ruling Congress.

When he took the oath as Vice President, Lyndon B. Johnson could understandably feel a glow of satisfaction. Not only did Texas provide the electoral votes that assured his party the Presidency, but it could fairly be said that it was Texans who supplied the setting for the inauguration. For the first time, the ceremonies took place on the new East Front of the Capitol, a kind of Cinemascope reproduction of the original done in aseptic white marble.

If Mr. Johnson's eyes wandered, he could detect a new Senate Office Building, a marble temple that befits the seat of empire. Not far away, a massive new House Office Building was rising from a Texas-size crater. Elsewhere in the city, the wrecker's ball was set to crunch against buildings near the Capitol and the White House, to clear the way for still more projects dear to his native state.

Mr. Johnson would have been forgiven a grateful glance at Speaker Sam Rayburn, his fellow proconsul from Texas. During their joint rule over Congress since 1955, much has already been done to make Washington suit the taste of Texas. Ultimately, up to $200 million may be spent on their program for giving the Capitol a gleaming new wardrobe of marble, and providing new comforts for the servants of the people. The scale of the program is awesome; the Third House Office Building alone will cost more than the Capitol and the three older office buildings combined—about $22 million more than the $51 million total cost for the four earlier structures.

Predictably, there have been objections from the public. Costly, flashy, and huge—these are the favorite words of horrified critics. But the dissent has been drowned out by the chug of bulldozers and the sound of pneumatic drills. Here, for the benefit of future archaeologists, is an inventory of the projects undertaken during the Rayburn-Johnson duumvirate.

I I

Early Rayburn: The East Front. The most spectacular project was the demolition of the old East Front of the

Capitol. Since the time of John Quincy Adams, the nation's Presidents have been sworn in on the portico of the East Front. But Speaker Rayburn found the old sandstone façade wanting, and used his gavel to pound through a $10 million renovation job.

In 1956, an obscure rider to the Legislative Appropriations Act authorized the extension of the East Front by 32½ feet, thus reviving from limbo an old scheme for "improving" the Capitol. Three reasons have been put forth for the change: (1) a supposed "flaw" in the building would be corrected by extending the façade and thus putting the dome in better perspective; (2) the old sandstone entrance was unsightly and unsafe; and (3) more office space was needed in the Capitol.

Architects, informed laymen, and patriotic societies were overwhelmingly in accord in replying (1) that the alleged flaw was a cherished feature of the building and that correcting it was akin to mending the crack in the Liberty Bell; (2) that repair and restoration were not only feasible but also less costly than the extension plan, since a Bureau of Standards study showed that the original sandstone was sound enough to be resurfaced; and (3) that while it was true the extension would yield extra offices, the added floor space would cost about $200 a square foot, compared with $20 a square foot in the average office building. The new space would be the most expensive, observed one architect, "since they paved the lobby of the Teller Hotel in Central City, Colorado, with gold."

Three times, in annual convention assembled, the American Institute of Architects deplored the change. The editors of the three major architectural magazines expressed scorn. Frank Lloyd Wright called it "absolutely incredible." Leading newspapers across the country were dismayed. And frequent thunderclaps emanated from the Daughters of the American Revolution: "Shall we destroy the evidence of the good taste of the Founding Fathers?"

But Speaker Rayburn did not budge. He was chairman of the Commission for the Extension of the Capitol, and his fellow members—including former Vice President Nixon and former Minority Leader of the Senate William F. Knowland—did not feel inclined to quarrel. Matters of taste were the department of J. George Stewart, Architect of the Capitol, who, notwithstanding his title, is not an architect at all but a lame-duck Congressman from Delaware. Aesthetic support was supplied by Roscoe P. DeWitt, an architect from Dallas, Texas, who was a leading consultant to Mr. Rayburn. Mr. DeWitt's portfolio of buildings includes the Sam Rayburn Library in Bonham, Texas, and a suburban store for the Nieman-Marcus Company in Dallas.

A few mavericks in the Senate, however, headed the dissenters, and a bill to block the project was introduced. The hearings on this bill were the first and only held on the East Front project. At one session, on February 17, 1958, the Capitol Architect informed his critics that plans for the extension "do not belong to the public" and "are not for publication." Douglas Haskell, editor of *Architectural Forum*, said he was perhaps "naive" but he always thought the Capitol "belonged to the people of the United States." No secrecy was involved, Mr. Stewart maintained. "It is the way things are done on the Hill."

A piquant example of the "way things are done" came the following May 27, when Mr. Rayburn made his first appearance as a speaker at the National Press Club in twenty-one years, expressly to defend his project. The Speaker said that bids would be let on the project "as soon as the noise settles down on the Hill." He contended that the extension had already been authorized and "I don't see any use to chew that old cud again." Even if the Senate tried to halt the project, Mr. Sam added, "I am going to hold we have already passed it."

Speaker Rayburn's prescience was uncanny. The noise settled; the Senate defeated the delaying bill; and on August 20, 1958, the Safeway Steel Scaffold Company of Bladensburg, Maryland, placed the low bid for the preliminary surgery on the Capitol. The new East Front, a shiny marble replica of the old, was ready for the 1961 inaugural, just as Mr. Rayburn had promised.

III

Archaic Johnson-Chavez: The New SOB. While Speakeı Rayburn was making his stand on the East Front, the Senate was already busy with its own building campaign. Under the aegis of Majority Leader Johnson and the Senate Office Building Commission, ground was broken on January 26, 1955, for the structure that later became known as "the Great White Goof on Capitol Hill." It was hexed from the start; astrologists noted that it was born under the sign of Capricorn (the goat).

In what became a familiar pattern, Capitol Architect Stewart returned again and again for additional funds. This provoked Senator Allen J. Ellender of Louisiana to say at one point, "I have served here for twenty-two years, and I have never seen an architect who found more things to do than Mr. Stewart. It is unending."

Mr. Stewart, startled, asked: "Is that in the way of a commendation?" The Senator drawled back, "You can take it that way if you want to. Whether it is right or wrong I don't know, but we are spending by the millions."

First there was the $2,800,000 needed for the new Senate subway system; then there was a request for $9,500,000 to remodel the old SOB (as the office is known); next came a $1,000,000 bill for new furniture for the new SOB; then came $965,000 to buy adjoining property to provide parking space for 285 cars; and then $625,000 to buy up the remaining space near the new building. All requests were approved except the $9,500,000, which was whittled to a pin-money $250,000 for remodeling old SOB suites.

However, costs have a way of rising, and as work went along it was necessary to return to the coffers for $200,000, because land values on parking space had risen; $293,000 for more furniture, and finally $750,000 to remedy various defects in the building. As a fillip, $5,000 was thrown in to buy two monster bronze plaques to immortalize those responsible for the new SOB.

When the new building made its debut in January, 1959, it proved to be an excellent example of what $26,000,000 (or more) can buy. The exterior is chaste white Vermont marble, but within there is an uneasy coexistence of some 20 varieties of stone, ranging from Ozark Rouge to Radio Black. Colors like peacock green, rosy pink, and glowing tangerine dance from the walls of the 42 suites, 12 committee rooms, TV studios, and ladies' lounges. As a *tâche de couleur*, one cherry-red armchair nestles in each suite next to sofas in nutty brown. Every Senator has a huge Mosler safe in which he can deposit his secret memoirs. Besides an auditorium for 500 and twin cafeterias seating 350 apiece, the building contains 36 rest rooms, 46 marble drinking fountains, 19 shower stalls, 32 service sinks, 129 public wash basins, and

205 Senatorial wash basins—it has, one newspaperman observed, "more pipes than a Chinese opium joint."

But no sooner had the Senators moved in than oaths began to darken the air. Nothing seemed to work—except the things that worked too well. Clocks halted, stuck at 9:45, because the hands were too heavy. Ghostly wails issued from what appeared to be loudspeakers. Mail chutes sucked letters from the sender's hand and sent them plummeting with such speed that they caromed off the fancy mail conveyors in the basement. Elevators became as capricious as constituents; ramps on the underground garage had to be rebuilt because the 1959 yacht-sized cars scraped their chassis. Because one contractor evidently forgot to leave a hole for the new subway, another contractor had to chop open a thick, tiled wall. The gadget-laden intercom system boomed like a foghorn, or croaked feebly and went dead. "You can hear a beep sound from 350,000 miles in space," grumbled Senator Warren Magnuson of Washington, "but you can't make yourself heard over a microphone six inches from your face."

All this culminated in the scandal of The Carpet. Some Senators felt that the elegant tile floor, costing $100,000, was too slippery, and they requested carpeting. This would have cost $150,000 more and would have entailed unhinging 600 doors in order to grind a half-inch of walnut from the bottom. But the more frugal-minded, led by Senator Paul Douglas of Illinois, won a compromise: carpets would be optional for those who wanted them. Fifteen Senators did; the bill to the taxpayers was a petty $53,550.

Architect Stewart and a swarm of helpers spent all that was needed to caulk the holes and mend the sails of the

Senate's golden galleon. In addition, Senators with holdings in other parts of the Capitol were generously compensated. Former Majority Leader Johnson wound up with a total of six suites scattered in the Capitol and the old and new SOBs. The Senate also secretly voted at one point to spend $40,000 assigned for "rusty plumbing" on a new swimming pool in the basement of the old SOB. The white-tile pool will be a handsome complement to the existing health suite, in which three *masseurs* are on hand to thwack Senatorial limbs.

Thus the Senate has become a citadel of comfort as well as rectitude, a place where members of the inner club can grump in snug surroundings about the decline of republican virtue. Full credit for this goes to Mr. Johnson and to Senator Dennis Chavez of New Mexico, chairman of the Senate Building Commission.

IV

Middle Rayburn: The Third HOB. Among Mr. Rayburn's many ten-gallon hats is the chairmanship of the House Building Commission, and in this capacity the Speaker kept a competitive eye on the upper chamber's steam shovels. Only a few months after the new SOB was under way, Mr. Rayburn found that *his* chamber's office buildings were cramped and inadequate. He advised the House Appropriations Committee that a $2 million starter was needed on a third office building, and four days later the House as a whole approved his plan. Phase two quickly followed as Architect Stewart announced plans for a $18.5 million program to remodel the existing House Office Buildings.

By the time the numbered House got around to debating the project, the foundation for the third HOB was already being dug. Nonetheless, an attempt was made on May 21, 1957 to strike out a $7.5 million appropriation for the new structure. Mr. Rayburn again took the floor and patiently explained that this would be "false economy," since excavations had begun.

Meanwhile, curiosity was expressed about what the new building would look like—and it was discovered in August, 1959, that no plans had yet been presented. By then, some $16 million had been spent on digging the biggest hole in town. Malicious rumors were circulating that the building would be a mile-high copy of the Alamo, done in pink bakelite.

Mr. Stewart's office reported that drawings were not available, but that Harbeson, Hough, Livingston & Larson of Philadelphia had prepared sketches which might be released some day. The Architect's aides did confide that the new building would be H-shaped, four stories high, and would contain 170 suites, 15 subcommittee rooms, and parking for 1,638 cars. As to cost, one breakdown lists $64,000,000 for construction, $2,500,000 for buying and clearing the site, $3,500,000 for architectural and engineering fees, $1,400,000 for a sewer to carry a creek beneath the building, and $750,000 for test borings and soil analysis. But prices are going up, and Representative H. R. Gross of Iowa may be right in predicting that the total cost will ultimately reach $82,000,000.

On October 15, 1959, a sketch was finally published. Critics said that the new building was in conventional Federalese, *i.e.*, without any discernible style. But whatever the harsh contemporary judgment, when the third HOB is completed by 1962 it will surely be a vintage example of Middle Rayburn, a suitable monument to the Builder from Bonham.

V

Judicial Rayburn: The Courthouse. Lafayette Square, a small public park in front of the White House, still possesses something of the sleepy charm of the capital's buggy and gaslight era. But, lamentably, not for long. Some of the old buildings surrounding the square have already been doomed as the site for a monster Executive Office Building. Most of the rest are about to be torn down to make way for a courthouse occupied by two Federal benches headed by judges from Texas.

Both the Court of Claims and the Court of Customs and Patent Appeals need more space. On this point there is no debate. But Chief Judge Marvin Jones and Chief Judge Eugene Worley have evidently determined that the only suitable site is on Lafayette Square, and on the side occupied by the Dolly Madison House, the Benjamin Tayloe House, and the old Belasco Theater.

When this plan was announced in 1960, the wholly expected public outrage forced the Senate to hold public hearings, with wholly predictable results. A host of civic organizations appealed to the sentiment and conscience of the Senate, and urged that the Belasco Theater (now used to store Treasury records) be rehabilitated as a functioning opera house, a facility that the major capital of the free world now lacks.

The citizens had the arguments; the judges had the potent birth certificates. Both judges are former Texas Congressmen, and Judge Jones also happens to be Sam Rayburn's brother-in-law. Congress approved the courthouse plan and sent it along to the White House, whose tenant at the time—as some noted with a touch of paranoia—was born in Denison, Texas.

VI

The yen to build, to "improve," to marbleize, is insatiable. First of all, it is a lot of fun. When the Senate installed a magnificent new subway system—as shiny as Moscow's—sleek subway cars, costing $75,000 apiece, were installed. On June 5, 1960, when the first equipment arrived, the baptismal ceremonies included a maiden race, à la Ben Hur, and a speech by Senate Chaplain Frederick Brown Harris, who dubbed the vehicles "swift chariots of democracy." The charioteers, it has been reported, may soon wear spiffy uniforms as they shuttle Senators to the dome.

Secondly, it is a way of dispensing immortality. One of Congress' early achievements in the Eisenhower years was to approve the construction of a memorial bell tower to Senator Robert A. Taft. Since then, plans for additional monuments have proliferated. One project is to build a vast Freedom Wall near Arlington National Cemetery. Memorial commissions are studying plans for monuments to Franklin Roosevelt, Theodore Roosevelt, Woodrow Wilson, and James Madison. Meanwhile, the city of Washington, which Congress governs, copes with shamefully inadequate schools.

But perhaps most important, the building binge is symptomatic of a deep-rooted legislative frustration. More and more power has gravitated to the White House, while Congress has lost some of its original importance as an architect of public policy. Thus if Congress cannot compete with the Executive as an initiator of legislation, it can compete as a consumer of marble. Like a householder furious with his more successful neighbor, Congress can still smash up the dishes in the kitchen.

A choice piece of crockery in the Capitol kitchen is the West Front. In a report dated August, 1957, Architect Stewart listed the extension of the West Front of the Capitol in a table of things-to-do. While the plan is now dormant, it is sure to be revived, because it envisages, as a sugarplum, yet another restaurant for members of Congress.

Then there is the proposal to extend the House and Senate wings on the Capitol's East Front in order to match the extension of the central portico. The plan has been urged by John F. Harbeson and Gilmore D. Clarke, both architectural consultants to Mr. Rayburn. Presumably, the purpose of the new extension will be to correct the "flaw" caused by the present prominence of the main portico.

Finally, there is a proposed new annex to the Library of Congress—a building which will contain more shelf-space than the present Library and annex combined. While the site of the new annex has not yet been chosen, Mr. Rayburn has moved with his usual alacrity to ensure that it will be abreast of his three House Office Buildings. In June, 1960, Mr. Rayburn announced that $5 million was needed to buy two blocks on Capitol Hill as a possible Library site. Within four days the House Appropriations Committee approved the request, pausing only long enough to hear Congressman John Rooney of New York term the property "ptomaine row," because the restaurants on the two blocks do not meet Mr. Rooney's culinary standards. Thus in the space of less than three weeks, several hundred shopkeepers and homeowners found their property doomed and their neighborhood derided as a breeding-place of disease. In its local dealings, Congress prefers the Big Stick to the Good Neighbor policy.

By and large, the White House has been indifferent to this building boom. It has been preoccupied with other matters—the art of projecting an image.

6 /

That Image in the White House

> You have shown me a strange image, and they are strange prisoners.
>
> Like ourselves, I replied; and they see only their own shadows, or the shadows of one another, which the fire throws on the opposite wall of the cave.
>
> True, he said; how could they see anything but the shadows if they were never allowed to move their heads? . . .
>
> To them, I said, the truth would be nothing but the shadows of the image.
>
> —PLATO, *The Republic*

IT MUST HAVE BEGUN in a flossy executive suite on Madison Avenue. The year was 1952, the subject was the latest account—a product named Eisenhower—and the momentous words might have been these:

"He's not penetrating, J. B. There's no smack, no punch, no consumer impact. What we've got to do is to crystallize a new . . . a new *image*."

And there it was. We've been stuck with the word ever since, and no political discussion seems authoritative without a respectful allusion to the candidate's image. It goes beyond politics. By now, everyone has discovered that everything has an image—from people and parties down to the lowly prune (depth interviews showed that the prune's image "was ridden with meanings, all unfortunate," according to Vance Packard).

The term has become so widely accepted that it seemed wholly in order during the 1960 campaign for an Associated Press profile of Richard M. Nixon to be subheaded "Man and Image"—with the undeniable implication that there was a difference between the two. Inevitably, Rabbi Max Nussbaum of Los Angeles opened the third session of the Democratic Convention by beseeching divine assistance for an "America with a new image." At the Republican Convention, images flew like hailstones—most memorably, perhaps, when the Governor of West Virginia retroactively endowed Lincoln with the "image of freedom."

During the campaign, the combatants hurled loaded images at each other. This came to a crescendo at the end of October, when President Eisenhower accused Candidate Kennedy of having "cruelly distorted the image of America." On the same day, the Washington *Post* quoted Mr. Kennedy's rejoinder: "Our prestige is not so high. No longer do we give the image of being on the rise. No longer do we give an image of vitality."

Political reporters vied with each other to find new and daring uses of the term. Chalmers M. Roberts of the Washington *Post* wrote that in agreeing to run together, Senators Kennedy and Johnson "broke the standardized image so many have of them." But what can be broken can be mended, and the same week columnist William S. White explained that Kennedy approached Johnson "and asked him to provide the cement so sorely needed— the image of a Protestant Southwesterner—so that the total image would not be solely that of a Catholic Easterner."

Cemented or broken, images come in a variety of shapes and sizes, are negative, bright or blurred, and even come in the big family-size package. The most basic of all images is the father image—the fellow who used to be in the White House. But coming up fast is the image of the sixties which was heralded in August of 1960 by a front-page headline in the Washington *Star*: "The Son You Vote For May Become President." So testified Dr. Martin Grotjahn, a psychiatrist at the University of Southern California, who found that Mr. Kennedy and Mr. Nixon "have remarkably similar images."

"Both appear as victorious sons," quoth the good doctor, "but they are also brothers, *alter egos* in a sense, to many middle-aged persons who feel 'I realize I cannot be President but my brother can.'"

Thus, among other distinctions, the 1960 election afforded the first instance of sibling image rivalry. But, with a bow to the growth issue, Dr. Grotjahn also held out this bipartisan consolation: "Of course, the son may grow later —in the voter's conception—into a benevolent father image the way Franklin Delano Roosevelt did."

II

At the risk of grievously damaging my own personalized image, I have consulted the dictionary to see what all the talk is about. The *Pocket Oxford Dictionary* scarcely affords comforting reading. An image by definition is a polite kind of fraud, a trick with mirrors, as well as a symbol or conception. The meaning of image (root: *imitari*, to imitate) is:

Imitation of object's external form, *e.g.*, statue esp. as

object of worship; form, semblance; counterpart; type; simile; metaphor; optical counterpart produced by rays of light reflected from mirror, etc.

Now the primary meaning clearly conveys the impression of humbug, and the final meaning suggests compellingly that an image is a deceptive optical illusion. Surely it is appropriate that the word image came into currency after the 1952 Presidential campaign introduced, in a big way, two miracle ingredients into politics: (1) advertising agencies, and (2) television.

The coincidence is revealing. An image, like an advertisement, is not the substance of an object but its ephemeral shadow; it is the beguiling package, not the reality within. Most important, in all its meanings an image connotes something contrived. Whether in the fine arts or the black arts, an image is a conceit, a concoction, a cabalistic device. Hence, in the familiar usages, images are "projected," "created," "updated," and even (see above) "standardized." The shaping of an image, then, is a technique of manipulation, not of reasoned persuasion.

Above all, the image is associated with visual presentation. In the years when radio was the chief tool of mass communications, there was little talk about images and a good deal of solemn discourse about the intangible quality known as "radio personality." The change came swiftly. In 1948, Thomas E. Dewey defeated Harold Stassen in the pivotal Oregon Presidential primary after a radio debate. In 1950, Governor Dewey market-tested television by centering his campaign for re-election on a carefully staged question-and-answer TV show. It worked. In 1952, General Eisenhower was the first candidate to be retailed nationally over television, chiefly through spot announcements. (Voice: "Mr. Eisenhower, can you bring taxes down?" Eisenhower: "Yes. We will work to cut billions in Washington spending and bring your taxes down.")

After the election, there was a heavy reliance on TV spectaculars. Bill Tyler, a columnist for *Advertising Agency*, wrote admiringly of one such performance in 1953:

> Undoubtedly the most effective commercial of the month was the President's TV appearance around the first of June. . . . It closely followed the pattern of an agency new-business solicitation. The President let each department head, armed with slides, present the story of his branch of the business. Then he wrapped the whole thing up in a masterful manner and asked for the order. As a TV salesman, we think you will agree that Dwight Eisenhower has few peers. . . .

But to connoisseurs, the campaign of 1956 was a letdown. This time the Eisenhower image presented new problems because of the President's illnesses. As pollster Louis Harris saw it: "Eisenhower is no longer looked on as being vigorous. Courageous he still is . . . but the image has mellowed. He is now looked on as being more kindly, wiser, and as one voter put it, 'kind of a grandfather to the republic.'" In addition, Adlai Stevenson could not adapt to the adman's approach, though he tried manfully, appearing on one spot announcement with a homey sack of groceries on his arm. This was no match for Ike and Mamie singing "God Bless America."

"I can't recall a national advertising campaign which was so poorly conceived, so badly written, so clumsily managed and produced, so misdirected and so dishonest as the political campaign of 1956," concluded John G. Schneider, author of *The Golden Kazoo* and an adman himself.

"Maybe if we get some smart, amoral, know-how boys into the act, we'll get a better show in 1960."

Mr. Schneider had his wish. We went from the mellow, kindly gramps from old Abilene to a college quiz show. Both candidates in 1960 sought exposure on TV in every possible way—filmed biographies, spot announcements, rallies, and debates—but Mr. Nixon was the more enterprising of the two. He wound up his campaign with "Dial Dick Nixon," a one-man telethon which reached new heights, or touched new depths, depending on your view. Mr. Nixon answered questions from viewers, chatted with his family and with movie stars, and heard fervent appeals for his election from Jinx Falkenberg and Ginger Rogers (who spoke for the *rentier* class in recalling that she too lived on a fixed income).

But Mr. Nixon, with a sure showman's instinct, sensed that too much floss and furs could blemish his image. "Let's cut the junk," he snapped at one point. "Let's just have questions for the next hour."

III

A good deal of the preoccupation with the image is of course pretense and fad, springing from an innocent desire to appear *au courant*. But there is more to it than that. It can be plausibly argued that the advent of the image is a symptom of potential corruption of our political system.

In essence, the assumption behind the talk about imagery is that appearance is far more important than substance. It is not whether the candidate *is* folksy, vigorous, experienced, and pious, but whether he *appears* to have those qualities. This is hardly an original doctrine; Machiavelli phrased it in its classic form four centuries ago when he advised that on occasion the Prince must be faithless, adding:

> But it is necessary to be able to disguise this character well, and to be a great feigner and dissembler; and men are so simple and so ready to obey present necessities, that one who deceives will always find those who allow themselves to be deceived. I will mention only one modern instance. Alexander VI did nothing else but deceive men, he thought of nothing else, and found the occasion for it; no man was ever more able to give assurances, or affirmed things with stronger oaths, and no man observed them less; however, he always succeeded in his deceptions, as he knew well this aspect of things. It is not necessary therefore for a prince to have all the above named qualities [*i.e.*, the conventional virtues], but it is very necessary to seem to have them.

What *is* startling is that this dissembling quality should now be treated as a matter of course—and that psychiatrists, theologians, and political writers should engage in solemn public autopsies on the candidate's phantom self. This is not only startling; it is alarming. It is a form of cynicism appropriate to the era of Charles Van Doren. The mere avowal of the paragraph quoted above, more than anything else, has made Machiavelli's name synonymous with guile. Today, one suspects, Niccolò would be a much-honored, much-quoted adviser to a Presidential candidate—as Murray Chotiner was, until his image slipped.

IV

In pragmatic political terms, too, the cult of the image has a disturbing implication. It is that a candidate's potential for the White House is measured not only by his true qualities but also by the astral personality he manages to project through a vacuum tube. The most convincing demonstration of the shortcomings of this approach can be made by taking an image inventory of Presidents past.

Let us begin in the approved IBM manner by turning the image into a statistical formula. Let us divide the image into seven components—manner, health, background, appearance, experience, viewpoint, and religion. In order for a candidate to compile a perfect score, he must: (1) appear to have an acceptably homey manner; (2) seem in robust health; (3) suggest a background of modest means; (4) look like a heroic marble bust; (5) possess an apparent record of extensive experience; (6) seem moderate in all his views; and (7) appear to be a model of Protestant piety.

It is a revelation to measure our Chief Executives by this standardized image yardstick. George Washington, for example, would score a meager four, because of his hopeless dentures, his insufficient informality, and his wealthy plantation background. John Adams would do little better, by virtue of his dubious Unitarian affiliation, his crochety personality, and his Harvard taint.

Jefferson's image rating is a dismaying three. His eccentric religious views, his immoderate espousal of liberty and revolution, his affluence, and his withdrawn, intellectual manner would hardly provide an image adequate to the election of a county coroner. Andrew Jackson might do a little better (4.5), but his abrupt manner, his gaunt and gnarled appearance, and his splenetic partisanship would give an account executive cause to reconsider.

Of all our Presidents, Lincoln has the most dismal image; it is obvious why Stephen Douglas trounced Lincoln in the race for the Senate (I would give Douglas a 6-plus). Odd-ball views on religion, an almost total lack of experience, rumors of illegitimacy, scarecrow appearance, melancholy disposition, an unfortunate ribald streak, *and warts*—all this adds up to what the PR boys would call a big nothing. One can hear the authentic voice of Madison Avenue: "J. B., there'd be a civil war if the Republicans put up that village crank."

Cleveland, of course, is automatically out of the running because he publicly admitted to fathering a bastard child, and Teddy Roosevelt is too bumptious, too toothy, too dogmatic, and too wealthy. Mark Hanna, who knew a good image when he saw one, spoke for the ages when he gasped, "Now look, that damned cowboy is President of the United States!" Wilson would get the same low rating (3.2) for the opposite reasons: too aloof, too highbrow, too frail-looking, too sanctimonious.

As for Franklin Roosevelt (4.9), the negative factors are physical infirmity, excessive wealth, and a Harvard degree. Harry Truman is impossible: a failure in business, immoderate language, flashy sport shirts—how he ever beat the superbly imaged Thomas E. Dewey (6.95) is matter for wonder.

On the other hand, if we peer backward, certain Presidents emerge with impeccable images:

James Buchanan: A muscular six-footer with an impressive record of experience (Secretary of State, Minister to Great Britain, Congressman), magnificent bearing, a stout Presbyterian.

Ulysses S. Grant: Humble origins, a salty virility, sound experience, a good Methodist, and—as a bonus—name well-known.

Rutherford B. Hayes: Stately appearance, with a reassuring patriarchal beard, moderate views, ample experience (Governor of Ohio), eight children, regular Methodist church-goer.

William McKinley: Stunning profile, impression of enormous vitality, sound and sane views, well-seasoned (Governor and Congressman), a pillar of Methodism.

Warren G. Harding: Handsomest President of this century, a staunch Baptist but with winning bonhomie, broad experience (Lt. Governor, Senator), sturdily moderate.

The clinching point is that all of these Chief Executives look far more impressive on a postage stamp than a Lincoln or Jefferson. It is strange that the Post Office Department relegates Harding and Buchanan to such exotic denominations as fifteen cents and two dollars.

Coming to the present, there can be little debate as to which of the two candidates in 1960 had the more salable image. Mr. Nixon's persona is marred only by a trace of Quakerism. Self-made, brimming with experience, prodigiously moderate, and as folksy as a Sears, Roebuck catalogue, Mr. Nixon deserves a respectable 6.54 rating. Then let us examine John Fitzgerald Kennedy: Controversial religious affiliation, callow appearance, a trace of arrogance in manner, the Harvard blot, millionaire background, an author. "He'll never do, J. B.," says a voice on the thirty-sixth floor, "with that corny New Frontier routine and that lover-boy look."

One wonders whether it is not time to halt this degrading game by burying the mischievously occult word. An appropriate epitaph might be the Commandment which, as you recall, warns the children of Israel: "Thou shalt not make unto thee any graven image. . . ."

7 /

Fortress of Yesterday

> And I reflected that if anything in Washington deserved
> such imperial housing, it was now the United States
> Supreme Court . . . it has survived to become today
> perhaps the most morally impressive of our original
> institutions.
>
> —EDMUND WILSON

O F ALL THE PARADOXES of contemporary politics,
none seems quite so baldly improbable as that involving
the Supreme Court of the United States. In the traditional
liturgy of the left, the Court was the citadel of privilege,
a place to be viewed with wary suspicion or outright hos-
tility. During the height of the New Deal fight over the
Supreme Court, Drew Pearson and Robert S. Allen complained bitterly, "It is easier to change the ruling head of
the European monarchal system, which we shook off, than
the Supreme Court's decree." And: "Curb the Court before it destroys the Nation," urged the liberal Philadelphia
Record in 1936. But twenty years later, virtually the identical words were being used by the spokesmen of the right.
The American Bar Association, which used to discuss the
Court in tones of hushed reverence, became so critical

that the Chief Justice of the United States resigned his membership. In Georgia, the State Legislature adopted a resolution demanding the impeachment of six Justices, and *Life* magazine scolded the Court for displaying the "most lamentable virginity about Communism."

Perhaps most remarkable of all was the changing attitude to judicial review. The power of the Supreme Court to nullify legislation was in time past regarded by radicals as the ultimate weapon of the propertied few. But now the Court is being chided for not using this power often enough in the field of civil liberties. And in 1960, Charles L. Black, Jr., one of the bright young liberals at Yale Law School, wrote a book hailing judicial review as a crowning achievement of the American democratic system.

This shift in opinion reflected a realignment of the three branches of government during the Eisenhower years. Inertia prevailed in the White House, Congress was stalled at dead center, and it was chiefly in the Supreme Court that the more bracing spirit of the New Deal seemed to survive. On two historic days—May 17, 1954 and June 17, 1957—the High Court directly confronted two controversies which the executive and legislative had been unwilling or unable to resolve. In *Brown* v. *Board of Education* the Court unanimously held that segregated public schools were repugnant to the Constitution, and in *Watkins* v. *U.S.* the Court placed new limits on the tactics of Congressional investigators.

Thus, nine men who can originate no laws and who can impose no taxes were able to use the negative power of review to give fresh vitality to the Declaration of Independence and the Bill of Rights. If one considers that President Eisenhower failed to give the Supreme Court effective support on its most controversial decision, the far-reaching change that has taken place since 1954 is all the more impressive. Whatever the difficulties of enforcement, there is broad approval for the desegregation decision. It is fair to say that the most significant social innovation in America during the post-war years was precipitated not by the President or by Congress but by what is supposedly our most venerable and conservative institution.

I I

The incongruity in outlook among the three branches of government is a familiar theme, because through much of our history the Supreme Court has been the fortress of yesterday. "The Court . . . is almost never a really contemporary institution," the late Justice Robert H. Jackson wrote:

> The operation of life tenure in the judicial department, as against elections at short intervals of the Congress, usually keeps the average viewpoint of the two institutions a generation apart. The judiciary is thus the check of a preceding generation on the present one; a check of a conservative legal philosophy upon a dynamic people, and nearly always the check of a rejected regime on the one in being.

But Mr. Justice Jackson overstated the point—the check is not necessarily that of a conservative legal philosophy on a liberal-minded government. It can be the other way around; a dynamic legal philosophy can predominate in the judiciary while a cautious conservatism prevails in the White House. Certainly this was the case during the Eisenhower years. There was more purposeful debate, more intellectual ferment, in the chambers of the Supreme Court than in either Congress or the White House. Somehow, the nine men in black seemed younger in spirit than those who governed from the cloakrooms and the golf course.

As far back as 1800, the function of the Court as an outpost of a defeated faction became apparent. Jefferson may have won the elections, but the defeated Federalists retained control of the judiciary, and Chief Justice John Marshall used the full force of his powers to enunciate his nationalist views and to assert the independence of the Court. After the doctrine of judicial review was first developed in *Marbury* v. *Madison*, Jefferson was appalled:

> The Constitution, on this hypothesis, is a mere thing of wax in the hands of the judiciary, which they may twist and shape in any form that they please. . . . A judiciary independent of the king or executive alone is a good thing; but independent of the will of the nation is a solecism, at least in a republican government.

The same complaint was again heard in the age of Jackson, when ardent Democrats were once more confronted by a Court led by Marshall and his new ally, Joseph Story, who despaired of democracy and proudly asserted, "I am a Whig." In 1835 Marshall died, and Jackson appointed as his successor a radical Democrat, Roger Brooke Taney, who lived on to administer the oath of office to President Lincoln. By this time the terms of controversy had changed, and Taney himself was the voice of a defeated faction, becoming progressively more crabbed and dogmatic in his views. Lincoln, like Jackson, was sardonically critical of his Chief Justice.

Following the Civil War, the Supreme Court had a brief moment of liberalism, notably in the Granger cases which upheld the regulatory rights of state governments. But during the long Republican era the High Court became steadily more concerned with the rights of business and more indifferent to the rights of man. This culminated in a series of opinions during the 1890's in which what are now the views of Barry Goldwater became the law of the land.

The function of the Court as the brake of yesterday can be clearly seen in the Income Tax case. In 1894, the agrarian revolt was at high tide, and a Populist-influenced Congress imposed a Federal income tax which touched the purses of the wealthy. Joseph H. Choate, a clever Philadelphia lawyer, was retained to combat the pernicious tax. He opened his final plea to the Court with a shocker:

> The Act of Congress which we are impugning before you is communistic in its purposes and tendencies, and is defended here upon principles as communistic, socialistic— what shall I call them—populistic as ever have been addressed to any political assembly in the world. . . . Now, if you approve this law, with this iniquitous exemption of $2,000, and this communistic march goes on and five years hence a statute comes to you with an exemption of $20,000 and a tax of 20 per cent upon all who have incomes in excess of that amount, how can you meet it in view of this decision my opponent asks you to render? There is protection now or never.

The Court was attentive. In a five-to-four decision, it ruled that the income tax was unconstitutional, and Mr. Justice Field, in a candid concurring opinion, lamented: "The present assault upon capital is just beginning." The conservative press was exultant. "The wave of the socialist revolution has gone far," said the jubilant New York *Sun*, "but it breaks at the foot of the ultimate bulwark set up for the protection of our liberties. Five to four the Supreme Court stands like a rock."

Two years later, in *Plessy* v. *Ferguson*, the Court pro-

claimed the separate-but-equal doctrine, thereby complet-
ing the retreat from the Civil War's legacy of radicalism.
Mr. Justice Harlan (who also delivered a forceful dissent
in the Income Tax case) vainly reminded his colleagues
that the Constitution is color blind. It took a constitutional
amendment to reinstate the income tax, and three generations to remove the stigma of color from the slogan of the
Supreme Court: "Equal Justice Under Law."

III

During this century, the Court has had its vicissitudes,
but it has rarely been a more impressive or interesting institution than under the leadership of Chief Justice Earl
Warren. Taken as a group, the Justices are men of exceptional character and force of conviction. Through the lucky
chance of Mr. Eisenhower's Court appointments, and
through the longevity of three towering Roosevelt appoint-
ees (Justices Black, Frankfurter, and Douglas), the Court
has been immune from the flabbiness and lethargy that
have otherwise been pandemic in our politics.

By and large, the old questions which used to crowd
the Court's docket—the definition of the Commerce clause,
the question of due process as a limitation on regulatory
powers—have been resolved in a broad Marshallian fashion.
What the nine Justices have also done is to hew out new
areas of controversy on the frontier of the law.

I write as a layman, without legal erudition. Yet around
us in Washington we can see the visible signs of the changes
the Supreme Court has wrought. Most readily apparent,
of course, is the desegregation of the Capital's public
schools, which, though it has entailed difficulties, has on
the whole been a model of enlightened reform. At a deeper

level, the school decision has altered the moral environment; it has contributed immeasureably to the steady elimination of the vestiges of *apartheid* in democracy's principal city.

Less widely appreciated, however, is the fact that we are able to see movies and buy books with less prior meddling by censors. One of the Court's signal achievements has been a series of decisions which have broadened the area of freedom at the bookstall and the theater.

One can also utter impudent opinions about Congressional investigators with the knowledge that, if ever one should be forced to appear before any self-appointed guardians of national security, there must be a demonstration of the pertinence of that appearance to some valid legislative purpose. Although there has been a considerable narrowing of the *Watkins* doctrine, four of the nine Justices remain implacably opposed to any dilution of the First Amendment.

Finally, as an intangible bonus, the Supreme Court has added the savor of controversy to the normally bland political news. Its bench is graced by two of the most formidable figures in the Capital, Mr. Justice Black and Mr. Justice Frankfurter, who, whatever their deep differences, share a power of intellect that has already left its impress on the law. Indeed, Justices Frankfurter and Black represent the best in the liberal tradition, and their continuing debate recalls the duality of the New Deal—Mr. Justice Frankfurter, urbane and erudite, the immigrant who is steeped in the New England tradition of Mr. Justice Holmes, a jurist who sees in procedure the essence of the law; and Mr. Justice Black, whose roots are agrarian and radical, and whose opinions are a study in forthrightness, in the relentless pursuit of first principles. The loss of either man would be grievous; they personify what Washington has been missing.

IV

The world of the Supreme Court is outwardly serene and smoothly ordered. When the nine robed Justices enter the courtroom on an "opinion Monday," there is a hush as the marshal—one of the few Government officials who wears a swallow-tail coat—repeats the traditional chant:

> Oyez, Oyez, Oyez! All persons having business before the Honorable, the Supreme Court of the United States are admonished to draw near and give their attention, for the Court is now sitting. God save the United States and this Honorable Court!

As the opinions are read, a clerk distributes copies to newspapermen. Sometimes, in a major case, there will be four or five separate concurrences and dissents, all involving fine shadings of argument. The wire-service reporter has scant time for reflection; he must hurriedly digest the complexities into a simplified news lead which will immediately be fed into the teletype machine.

Errors in reporting, sometimes fundamental, have resulted, and this has led to periodic suggestions for reform. But the Court has resisted any suggestion of change. In a stolidly old-fashioned way, the Justices persist in thinking that it is not their job to facilitate the work of the press. The ultimate heresy is that the Court is the only major agency of government that does not employ a single full-time publicity man. There is a press room of sorts, and there is an official who distributes the opinions—but he is not empowered to speak for the Court and no handouts are proffered to the impatient press.

Change is the law of life, however, and it is a portent of the Court-to-come that one Justice has already suggested that the Court alternate between afternoon and morning on its "opinion Mondays," in order to show judicial impartiality as between the morning and afternoon newspapers. The Justice was new to the Court, and the reception he received must have been profoundly discouraging. But when the Smooth Jurists arrive in force, the hum of the mimeograph machine and the TV cameras may even invade the fortress of yesterday.

It could come about something like this. . . .

FROM: Ostby, Kohler, Brown & Wormgood, Public Relations Consultants
TO: The Chief Justice of the United States
RE: Humanizing the Court

It is with great reluctance that our firm has undertaken your assignment. The incessant controversy over the Supreme Court is indicative of a low level of public acceptance brought about by the shamefully primitive information program of the judiciary. Everywhere our associates have turned, we have been confronted by the same melancholy facts: a stuffy restrictiveness with regard to the press, a neglect of poll techniques, and a failure to gain maximum exposure through a scientifically-programmed media campaign.

Nonetheless, out of a sense of public service, we have accepted your assignment. Certain preliminary conclusions can be placed in sharp outline:

One. The question of dissents. It seems to us a wholly undesirable procedure for the Court to speak with many voices in public, and to air its differences in the open. . . .

Inevitably, the dissents puzzle the public and project an image of irresolution. Of course the Brethren have different opinions. But isn't it possible to thrash these matters out in sensible seclusion? And wouldn't it be better to omit all names on opinions, so that the Court could speak with vigorous oneness?

Two. The secrecy phobia. We live in an age when the public wants to know its Justices as whole men, not merely as stiff cardboard figures in a robe. The Court has been altogether negligent about exploiting its greatest natural resource: the warm, human qualities of its Justices. The wholesome home life of each Justice ought not be hidden from view. Let the Court initiate a systematic program of TV appearances, prepared anecdotes, and interviews for the magazines the housewife reads. A suggestion: Why not encourage the Justices to bring their wives and children to watch on important "opinion Mondays"?

Three. The horse-and-buggy courtroom. Your Court deals not only with cold, abstract problems—but also with people and all their homely foibles. But the public is presented only with arid opinions, drained of life and spirit. Why not offset this by permitting the televising of Court hearings? Everybody loves a courtroom drama, and with a little sprucing-up the present chambers could provide a suitable format. And when a case involves a lurid offense, why rely on secondhand testimony? Why not use film-clips that show the scene of the crime, the faces of bereaved relatives, etc.?

Four. Those opinions. Our immediate recommendation is that the Court begin by dressing up its opinions in a way simpler for the press to handle and the public to grasp. We submit these examples of what can be done:

OLD AND STODGY

WHY NOT REDESIGN ON TWO-COLOR LETTER HEAD, WITH PIX OF COURT AND SUITABLE SLOGAN?

SUPREME COURT OF THE UNITED STATES

CUTTING *v.* BANK OF ALASKA, ETC., ET AL.

APPEAL FROM THE UNITED STATES COURT OF APPEALS FOR THE NINTH CIRCUIT.

No. 925, Misc.   Decided June 27, 1960.

CAN'T WE JUNK THIS STUFF?

JARGON! PER CURIAM.

The appeal is dismissed. The motions for other relief are denied.

WHO? WHAT? WHEN? WHERE? WITHOUT FACTS, IT LOOKS AS IF THE COURT IS DUCKING THIS ONE.

*NO — RELEASE TIME
TELEPHONE NUMBER OF SOURCE
BIOGS OF JUDGES*

[handwritten: DEAD! DEAD! DEAD!]

No. 342.—October Term, 1959.

Howard L. Nostrand and Max Savelle, Appellants, *v.* Herbert Little, et al.	On Appeal From the Supreme Court of the State of Washington.

[handwritten: STICK IN BODY]

[May 2, 1960.]

[handwritten: WHAT MEANS?]

Per Curiam.

[handwritten: OPINION FIRST, FACTS LATER]

Washington requires every public employee to subscribe to an oath that he is "not a subversive person or a member of the Communist Party or any subversive organization, foreign or otherwise, which engages in or advocates, abets, advises, or teaches the overthrow, destruction or alteration of the constitutional form of the government of the United States, or of any political subdivision of either of them, by revolution, force or violence; . . ." Refusal so to do "on any ground shall be cause for immediate termination of such employee's employment." *

Appellants brought this declaratory judgment action claiming the Act to be violative of due process as well as other provisions of the Federal Constitution. One of the

[handwritten: KILL! WHO READS FOOTNOTES?]

*Chapter 377, Laws of Washington 1955. The pertinent part of that statute reads:

"Sec. 1. Every person and every board, commission council, department, court or other agency of the State of Washington or any political subdivision thereof, who or which appoints or employs or supervises in any manner the appointment or employment of public officials or employees . . . shall require every employee . . . to state under oath whether or not he or she is a member of the Communist Party or other subversive organization, and refusal to answer on any grounds shall be cause for immediate termination of such employee's employment . . . ."

The Washington Supreme Court construed this statute as requiring the element of *scienter*.

[handwritten: WHAT MEANS?]

2 NOSTRAND *v.* LITTLE.

claims is that no hearing is afforded at which the employee can explain or defend his refusal to take the oath. The Supreme Court of Washington did not pass on this point. The Attorney General suggests in his brief that prior to any decision thereon here, "the Supreme Court of Washington should be first given an opportunity to consider and pass upon" it. Moreover, appellants point to a recent case of the Washington Supreme Court, *City of Seattle* v. *Ross*, 154 Wash. Dec. 794 (adv. sheets), 344 P. 2d 216 (1959), as analogous. There that court overturned an ordinance because it established a presumption of guilt without affording the accused an opportunity of a hearing to rebut the same. In the light of these circumstances we cannot say how the Supreme Court of Washington would construe this statute on the hearing point.

THIS IS WHAT LOSES READERS

The declaratory nature of the case, the fact that the State's statute here under attack supplements previous statutory provisions raising questions concerning the applicability of the latter, together with the comity that should be afforded the State with regard to the interpretation of its own laws, bring us to the conclusion that we must remand the case for further consideration. Cf. *Williams* v. *Georgia*, 349 U. S. 375 (1955).

Vacated and remanded. *HUH?*

THIS DECISION FLIES IN THE FACE OF POLLS WHICH SHOW COMMUNISM IS HATED. WHY NOT UPHOLD THE OATH? WHY NOT TRY FOR AFFIRMATIVE HEADLINES: "HIGH BENCH FLAYS RED CONSPIRACY"?

SUPREME COURT OF THE UNITED STATES

No. 36.—October Term, 1959.

Carl C. Inman, Petitioner,
v.
Baltimore & Ohio Railroad Co.

On Writ of Certiorari
to the Supreme Court
of the State of Ohio.

FIRST NAME?
INITIAL?

[December 14, 1959.]

Mr. Justice Frankfurter.

CAN'T THIS KIND OF THING BE SETTLED IN PRIVATE?

The opinion of my Brother Clark demonstrates, insofar as demonstration is possible in law, that this case should never have been brought here. In accordance with the views that I expressed in *Rogers* v. *Missouri Pacific R. Co.*, 352 U. S. 500, 524 (1957), and in which I have since persisted, the appropriate disposition would be dismissal of the writ of certiorari as improvidently granted. If these views were enforced under the special circumstances of this case, affirmance by an equally divided Court would result. Thereby this case would be cast into the limbo of unexplained adjudications, and the lower courts, as well as the profession, would be deprived of knowing the circumstances of this litigation and the basis of our disposition of it. Since I have registered my conviction on what I believe to be the proper disposition of the case, it is not undue compromise with principle for me to join Brother Clark's opinion in order to make possible a Court opinion.

CLOTS PACE

HOW ABOUT STATISTICAL REVIEW OF HOW MANY CASES DECIDED SO FAR, COMPARED WITH LAST YEAR?

8 /

The Soothing Cassandras

As the reporters in Washington survey the product
of all their labor, the honest ones sometimes feel
despairingly that more and more is being written about
less and less.

—DOUGLASS CATER

IN NO PROFESSION DOES DISTANCE lend so much enchantment as in journalism. The reader in Dubuque who picks up his local paper can be forgiven for conjuring up a flattering image of the Washington correspondent. He reads of mysterious "informed sources" who "reliably report" that a "sweeping new Congo policy" may "check the pro-Communist infiltration among Baluba tribesmen." Inevitably, there is the suggestion of whispered state secrets, an exchange of knowing looks in a hushed chancery, the shuffle of dispatch cases.

Then our reader in Dubuque turns to his favorite Washington columnist, and he feels as if he is in direct contact with the fonts of power. The column has a polished surface, and by skillful indirection conveys an impression of authoritative judgment. The reader is informed that "it is well understood" by those on the inside that the Congo

policy change "involves a calculated risk" of Western prestige which must be weighed against a continuance of "drift
and inertia." There are some signs, the columnist notes, of
a "bold new departure," which, however, only will look
bolder and may in the end find the nation where it was
before.

So, with a contented sigh, our reader folds up his paper
with the comforting impression that he has encountered
some useful new facts and lively judgments—when, in
truth, it just might be possible that the news article contained more official opinion than fact, and the column
contained no opinions but a carefully balanced set of statements which cancel each other out. Note: I say it *could* be
—in the best Washington tradition, one must add that
diplomatic circles, which in the past have proved authoritative, indicate that in some circumstances this might
roughly be the case. But, on the other hand. . . .

I I

The demigods of the press seem very mortal at closer
view, and no one takes greater delight in mocking the pre-
tensions of journalism than the working newspaperman.
Publishers, needless to say, are as solemn as archbishops
about their craft. But the reporter, possibly because he is
underpaid, thrown in the constant company of his own
kind, and exposed to the seamy side of his calling, draws
a psychic bonus in the form of intramural iconoclasm.

For example, the thoughtful reporter knows that the
traditional stereotype of the "yellow press" is an engaging
myth. The press today is uncompetitive, consolidated, and
respectable; it is less yellow than gray. In *Martin Chuzzle-
wit,* Dickens described the excesses of another era. Martin

and his friend Mark Tapley were leaving their ship in New York harbor when their ears were assailed by a chorus of newsboys:

Here's this morning's New York *Stabber!* Here's the New York *Family Spy!* Here's the New York *Private Listener!* Here's the New York *Peeper!* . . . Here's the full particulars of the patriotic loco-foco meeting yesterday, in which the whigs was so chawed up. . . . Here's the *Sewer's* exposure of the Wall Street Gang, and the *Sewer's* exposure of the Washington Gang, and the *Sewer's* exclusive account of a flagrant act of dishonesty committed by the Secretary of State when he was eight years old, now communicated, at great expense, by his own nurse.

But if Dickens recently had returned to the United States on a State Department leader grant, he might have found that the dear old *Sewer* had by accretion become the New York *Sewer-Peeper-Stabber & Family Spy*—a sonorous epitaph in Gothic type—and that the headlines sang a more muted song: "Trip Cancellation Hailed as Communist Setback," "Prestige Never Higher, Hagerty Says," "Herter Issues Unity Call," "Pro-Western Forces In Laos Hurl Back Red Invaders," and "President Rests in Augusta; Vetoes 'Spending Bill.'"

These, at any rate, were the kind of headlines to which Americans grew accustomed during the Eisenhower years, a period when we had the closest thing to an official press that the country had ever seen. To some extent, the uplift tone reflected a transient alliance between a Republican Administration and a predominantly Republican-owned press. But the headlines were also the mirror of a gradual change in the relationship of the press to officialdom—a change best summed up in the title of Douglass Cater's perceptive book, *The Fourth Branch of Government.*

Mr. Cater, Washington correspondent for *The Reporter*, points out that in our system of divided powers, the press acts as a broker and middleman to an extent not true of other democracies. But there is an added dimension to which he alludes. Due to the increased size and scope of Government, the reporter can no longer confirm the accuracy of a story by a conscientious firsthand check—often he becomes the captive of an official source. There are now an estimated 3,000 Government information officers —or twice the total of the Washington press corps itself. Thus, willy-nilly, the press has become entangled in the web of government, and the reporter on occasion may become a spokesman for an agency, a department, or a branch of Government.

But the dice are weighted against the journalist. Government secrecy complicates his task, deadline pressure is insistent, and he frequently can see the story only in fragments. And through long experience, the shrewder officials are aware of the conventions of the press and may adroitly exploit a reporter who is bound by the conventions of the wire-service news formula. The case of Joe McCarthy is the most spectacular example of how an unscrupulous politician can parlay bogus stories into headlines, because what a Senator says is "news," because reporters are inhibited from inserting evaluative opinions, and because time may be lacking to check before filing. But more insinuating is the way that the official "slant" creeps into routine stories filed from Washington and from abroad.

Take the case of Laos. On January 4, 1961, Arthur Dommen of UPI cabled this dispatch from Vientiane:

Communist-led Laotian rebels claimed Tuesday night they had recaptured the key central Laotian town of Xien

Khouan in a major victory and sent spearheads driving toward southern Laos. While the Communists were reporting new successes, King Savang Vathana dealt them a major diplomatic and propaganda setback by convening Parliament for a three-day session to invest pro-Western Boun Oum as Premier.

The tone is typical of much foreign reporting and clearly discloses the failing of misplaced concreteness so prevalent in American news stories. For this, reporter Dommen is not wholly to blame. His story was probably processed in this country—meaning an originally hopped-up dispatch was even further hopped-up so that the wire service could get the front-page play that is regarded as the measure of success. In stories of this kind, "howling mobs" always "hurl" shouts at the American Embassy, battles "rage," guns "thunder," and attacks "blister." As the following weeks revealed, nothing so sensational or definitive was at that moment happening in troubled Laos.

Second, the dispatch fits into the hard-news formula, *i.e.*, it wrests from the day's events something that sounds specific and new and states it in language used to report police court trials and county politics. The trouble is that the formula assumes that the reader is fully aware of the background, as indeed he usually is in the case of a local happening. In the case of Laos, the formula is misleading to the extreme. As we have gradually come to learn, Laos is really not a "nation," its political factions are really not "parties," and its government is not a "parliament"—at least not in the way these words are commonly understood in America.

Third, the dispatch is replete with official bias. Again, the reporter may not be completely at fault. It was probably censored, even though there is not even the slightest suggestion in the story that this might be the case. But the characterization of factions might be the same, censors or no, because the hard-news formula seems to demand an easily grasped good-guy, bad-guy rhetoric. Our faction is "pro-Western," the other fellows are "pro-Communist"— but, as we have learned to our grief in following events in Iraq, Egypt, Indonesia, Lebanon, and the Congo, labels like these have a way of becoming quickly unstuck. A modest reform has been suggested: Why not use the phrases "American-supported" or "Russian-supported" to characterize regimes—instead of pro- or anti-Western?

All this is well-understood in Washington, where there is a frustrated realization that the conventional techniques of journalism are inadequate to the new demands. Abler members of the press often look with envy on the European correspondents in the Capitol, who are allowed far greater latitude in expressing their opinions and who are encouraged to write essays rather than to fire a series of supercharged pellets at the reader. Doubtless the European tradition has its own shortcomings, but the American system of reportage has exalted "readability" (*i.e.*, short sentences that even the village idiot can understand) to the point of diminishing return. And by insistence on misplaced concreteness, the conventional formula opens the way to official manipulation by backstage briefing officers.

Small wonder that there is a bipartisan tendency among some high officials to regard the press literally as a fourth branch of government. When Secretary of State Dulles used his power to deny reporters access to Red China, the unspoken assumption was that the press was an agency of government and could be used for bargaining purposes in dealing with a foreign power. On that point at least, Mr.

Dulles and Peking were in momentary agreement. Former Assistant Secretary of State Andrew Berding gave a more explicit statement of the same philosophy in a speech to a group of newspapermen on November 18, 1960. The Associated Press reported:

> Mr. Berding said American information media have increasing responsibility for the "image of the United States" as it appears to foreign peoples. Mr. Berding, himself a former newsman, deplored "the scandal type of news" which he said foreign newspapers receive from American sources and publish. . . . He accused newspapers of publishing secret Government documents without raising any "excuse or explanation" about "whether it was right or wrong to do so." Mr. Berding also declared that some correspondents "concentrate on stories that show the Government in a bad light."

However, the speech was given in an unfortunate city. Mr. Berding spoke in Williamsburg, once the colonial capital of Virginia, where His Majesty's Royal Governors were also irritated by the habit of newspapermen to report stories that show the government in a bad light. One colonial Governor blurted in 1671: "I thank God we have no free schools nor printing. . . . For learning has brought disobedience and heresy and sects into the world; and printing has divulged them and libels against the government. God keep us from both."

III

But God failed the Royal Governor, and the devilment of print came to the colonies, sowing heresy and disobedience. Not long after the Revolution, in 1793, the first columnist made his appearance: Royall Tyler, a novelist and dramatist who wrote for the New Hampshire *Journal*, and who was the forefather of a garrulous and distinguished family.

Our columnists have acquired greater importance as the editorial columns of most newspapers have succumbed to what Louis Lyons calls "a conforming to conservatism that has become so habitual as to be unconscious." A press without Walter Lippmann, Joseph Alsop, James Reston, Murray Kempton, Marquis Childs, and their brethren would be barren indeed. Even the old curmudgeons of the right, George Sokolsky, David Lawrence, and Westbrook Pegler, are welcome abrasives in an age of slickness (though Mr. Sokolsky has mellowed so much that recently he even had a kind word for Dean Acheson).

Yet different times bring new styles, and there seems to be a distinct contrast between the generations of commentators. The old-timers boil with indignation; the new breed simmers in irony. The modern columnist tends to view his role as that of a drama critic who must help inept players to understand the script. The credo has been set forth by Richard Rovere, *The New Yorker's* shrewd political observer, in the preface to his book, *The Eisenhower Years:*

> . . . I do not look upon myself as a partisan or upon this book as a polemic. In general, my effort has been to write about politics as much as possible in the manner of a critic making an effort, as Matthew Arnold put it, "to see the object as in itself it really is." I believe that it is theoretically possible to bring to public affairs the sympathy, interest, hope, objectivity, and rigorous discrimination that a conscientious critic brings to literature, painting, music, architecture, or any other form.

The popularity of the Rovere approach is reflected in the changing aspirations of the young reporter. During the 1920's, the idol of the city room novice was probably H. L. Mencken; during the New Deal it was most likely Heywood Broun; at present the baton has passed to James Reston, the distinguished correspondent for *The New York Times*. Mr. Reston, whose antennae are among the most sensitive in his craft, himself remarked on the changing traditions of journalism in May, 1958, in a collective obituary for Elmer Davis, Thomas L. Stokes, Frank Kent, H. L. Mencken, Geoffrey Parsons, Herbert Elliston, Anne O'Hare McCormick, and Bernard DeVoto. "They differed from one another, this group, in manner, style, and political philosophy," Mr. Reston wrote, "but they resembled each other more than they resembled their successors. They were more outspoken than the modern breed. They were more reflective. They could write more vivid prose, and above all they had more wit and humor in their style."

Mr. Reston was generous to the old-timers, and perhaps too harsh on the successors. But nonetheless a change is evident. Thomas L. Stokes, a committed New Dealer, was succeeded in his column by William S. White, an able *New York Times* reporter, who summed up his view in a magazine article:

> The Eisenhower Administration cannot be made out, on any fair estimate, to be in any way evil. But its lack of evil is no less marked than its lack of taste. This is said wholly without malice, because I look upon politics simply as a profession or an art like painting and music; consequently, I have few political villains and no outright heroes.

I V

This aesthetic approach to political commentary has its strengths: literacy, fairness, and dry wit. Instead of the hammer, men of the new school use the nail-file—frequently with devastating results. But the shortcoming is that, all too often, gloomy private convictions end up in a far more comforting form in newsprint. The stress on fairness can act as a filter-chamber in which the complexity of an event is so carefully attended to that the judgment is left out.

It sometimes seems that the reader has to bring to political commentary the critical apparatus required for studying a stanza of Yeats or Eliot. Somewhere, tucked in all those words, there may be an opinion that can be discovered. The task is rendered more difficult by the fact that what appears to be a judgment often, on closer examination, turns out to be an evasion.

Over the years, I have learned to detect (and I confess, imitate) certain strategies for avoiding a judgment while seeming to express one. For convenience and brevity, I have distilled the devices into the Four D's: Dichotomy, Distribution, Description, and Displacement. Let us look at them one by one.

(1) *Dichotomy.* This technique is simple and can be easily mastered. It consists of taking a controversy and stating the opposing views in such a way as to imply that the truth lies somewhere in between—without, of course, identifying this "somewhere" more precisely. For example, here is a leading Washington commentator's assessment in 1956 of President Eisenhower's first term: "In summary, the Eisenhower Administration, like most of its predecessors, has been neither as ineffective as its opponents claim

nor as wise, imaginative, or successful as its skillful propagandists assert." And this is a Washington columnist's appraisal of the prestige issue in the 1960 campaign: "Our international political situation may not be as glamorous as indicated by Mr. Nixon, but it certainly is not as somber as described by Mr. Kennedy."

(2) *Distribution.* With practice, it is possible to find a common element of gain or loss for all contenders in a controversy, and then evenly to parcel out bouquets or brickbats. But it is important not to state explicitly who won the most or lost the most. As an example, this is the final sentence of one Washington columnist's post-mortem of the 1960 Presidential primary in Wisconsin: "On balance, it seems to me that Wisconsin has not helped any candidate very much and has hurt all of them somewhat." Or, another commentator's survey of the ruins of the Paris summit: "The whole thing is not a 'victory' for anybody. . . . It is a serious defeat for the President. . . . It is a serious defeat for Prime Minister Macmillan. . . . It is a serious defeat for Mr. Khrushchev and his policy of coexistence."

(3) *Description.* Skillfully handled, it is possible to describe a situation in such a way that it appears a crisp judgment has been rendered. Consider this concluding paragraph of a profile of James Hagerty in a leading news magazine:

> Hagerty has been accused at times of doing his job too well, of creating the image of a President more vigorous than he actually is, and thereby lulling the U.S. into a false and dangerous sense of complacency. But Press Secretary Hagerty cannot by the nature of his job manufacture a presidential record. He can only reflect what President Eisenhower does in its best light. In his ability to do just

that, James Campbell Hagerty, first of the professional press secretaries, may never be surpassed.

This seems straightforward enough; but the appearance of solidity dissolves at the touch. The first sentence raises a pointed charge: that Hagerty is doing his job too well, with harmful results. By a facile shift, the conclusion fails to address itself to this question but substitutes instead a description that is true of any press officer: he is paid to put his boss in the best light. The question of whether Hagerty, by doing so, has fostered a dangerous complacency, is left hanging—yet a quick reading conveys the impression that a sharp verdict has been delivered.

(4) *Displacement.* This consists of taking a lamentable situation and then assigning the blame in so diffuse a manner that no one, really, is responsible. Congress, the voters, the older generation, the younger generation, and the people in general are ideal scapegoats. For example, a Washington commentator recently surveyed his calling and found that our national reporting is too timid and too lacking in harsh candor. There is, he finds, an excess of togetherness, and a tendency among journalists to lump men and causes into some "shapeless generality." Then, with an eye for the hedges, the writer concludes: "But is this not a national, and not merely a Washington failing?" There is safety in numbers.

V

Let us conclude by wrapping all four D's into a single, all-purpose column. Suppose that a President unexpectedly offered to swap Alaska for East Germany to ease the cold war. Our columnist at the footlights would be ready with description, dichotomy, distribution, and displacement, in that order. Here might be the result:

WASHINGTON, February 29—The feeling in this city is that the President has given a new twist to the tired formulas of foreign policy by his bold proposal to exchange the state of Alaska for the East German People's Republic.

But despite the predictable outcry that has followed the President's carefully worded statement, the move is neither so ruinous as opponents contend nor as inspired a masterstroke as the Administration's publicists insist.

There would be gains and losses for both sides. Although the area of freedom would be extended to East Germany, the swap would also mean that the Soviet Union would acquire new bases near our defense perimeter, absorbing in the process the people of Alaska.

To an objective observer, the controversy over the President's proposal plainly provides another melancholy example of how the methods of diplomacy lag so sadly behind the needs of the atomic age. Surely such complex negotiations might best be carried on quietly by skilled specialists. At the same time, the necessity for secrecy—and the failure to brief the press—has meant that the public has been caught unawares, and a controversy damaging to unity is likely to follow.

VI

But we must proceed one step further, lest this survey itself seem to end without a judgment. How well does the American press serve its readers? Does the truth have a proximate chance to emerge from the pages of the typical paper? These are formidable questions, and it requires a degree of presumption to offer an answer. Yet since the virtues of our press are so insistently reiterated, the attempt ought to be made.

On the credit side, there seems little doubt that the reader is confronted with a greater volume of reportage on more subjects than ever before; he is nearly suffocated in newsprint. And it is worth stressing that there is less of a chasm between the "popular" press and the "quality" press here than in other countries; the New York *Daily News* carries more information than its tabloid counterpart in London.

But what about meaning? Does the typical Washington and foreign dispatch present a comprehensible picture of reality? Only an incurable optimist could argue the affirmative, without severe qualifications. We have examined the case of Laos, on the other side of the globe. Cuba is only ninety miles from United States soil, and yet few major news stories have been so clumsily handled as the Cuban Revolution. During the Batista years, wire-service stories from Cuba were colored by the flavor of official handouts in Havana. In the very last days of the Batista regime, this was the tone of the characteristic UPI dispatches:

> Cuban rebels claimed tonight that their advance patrols had entered the city of Santa Clara. . . . The rebel announcement came after a day in which President Fulgencio Batista hurled an almost steady stream of warplanes against rebel-held towns in Las Villas Province, in what appeared to be a major attempt to smash the two-year-old revolt.

This was filed from Havana on December 29, 1958, by Francis L. McCarthy—two days before the complete collapse of the Batista regime. Yet, while rebels "claim" victory, Batista "hurls" streams of warplanes. One reason for this discrepancy is that both wire services covered the Cuban civil war almost exclusively from Havana, and little attempt was made to get reporters into rebel areas. A possible explanation was lack of enterprise; another was fear of offending Batista because dictators have a way of throwing uncooperative press services out of the country—and both AP and UPI had lucrative franchises among the Havana papers. In any event, at the moment when the Batista regime was cracking apart and Cuban society in a state of near-disintegration, wire-service reports conveyed the impression of a forceful government welcoming a showdown with a handful of pesky rebels. Indeed, on the very eve of Castro's victory, one wire service was cabling accounts of Batista's supposed triumphs in Santa Clara. It does no good to blame it all on censorship, because, as in Laos, the stories themselves rarely indicated that they were subject to censorship.

After the downfall of Batista, attention swerved to the rebel firing squads, in no small part because executions find an easy echo in a hard-news lead. The equally important story—that Cuba was in the beginning stages of a profound social revolution—slipped through the sieve. By and large American readers had little idea of the rottenness of the old order or the widespread desire for fundamental change. Ultimately, some glimmerings of this reached the North American public, but by that time the Cuban insurgents who had been swiftly, and perhaps prematurely, called pro-Communists had become that in fact.

Thus, the reader could find a concise tabulation of how many victims had fallen before the firing squads—but no comparable statistics on the extent to which United States investors controlled the Cuba of old, or on the life-expectancy of a *guajiro* who lived in debased poverty on a rich island. In Cuba, as in Laos, the same melancholy process could be detected: hopped-up crisis reporting, facile labeling of adversaries, lack of perspective, and reliance on official sources. Only after weeks of near-hysterical reporting from Laos did readers learn that invasions were easier to describe than to confirm, and that the official U.S. version of events was subject to serious challenge. In the end, even the experts in *Realpolitik* at *Time* had to concede that the Laos crisis was a muddle of ambiguities.

The shortcomings of press reports from Africa, Asia, Latin America, and the Middle East reflect the changes in the post-Stalinist world when no bloc—even the Communist bloc—is glacially solid. More than ever, questions of mood and nuance are vital, and it is precisely in this area that the supercharged lingo of wire-service reports is most vulnerable. In the European press, where impressions are as important as "hard news," and where the words of U.S. briefing officials are given less than scriptural weight, a markedly different picture of events in places like Laos and Cuba is available. All too often, wire services inadvertently mislead by concealing the soft center to the "hard" news.

A different problem is posed by the vendors of opinion who could offer a corrective to the news columns by calling a trowel a trowel. One can understand, in view of the complexity of events, why a pundit would want to clothe a judgment in language of caution. But the traditional argument for free speech, as formulated by John Stuart Mill, assumed that the collision of strong opinion provided the best mechanism for arriving at the truth. The beneficiary of hard-hitting controversy, Mill contended, was not the impassioned participant but "the calmer and more disinterested bystander." Mill was less concerned by the "violent conflict of parts of the truth" than by the quiet suppression of half of it, because "there is always hope when people are forced to listen to both sides; it is when they attend to one that errors harden into prejudice, and truth itself ceases to have the effect of truth, by being exaggerated into falsehood."

So reasoned Mill; surely he would be troubled by a tradition of political commentary which seeks to express the consensus rather than criticize it. No matter how fair-minded the new school of pundits may be, their excessive emphasis on detachment may—paradoxically—prejudice the broader purpose of discovering the truth. There is a maxim by G. K. Chesterton which puts the matter astringently: "The angry historians see one side of the question. The calm historians see nothing at all, not even the question itself."

Part Two / Sources

9 /

From Melting Pot to Pressure Cooker

> What then is the American, this new man? He is
> either an European or the descendant of an European;
> hence that strange mixture of blood you will find in no
> other country. . . . Here individuals of all nations are
> melted into a new race of man.
>
> —MICHEL-GUILLAUME DE CREVECOEUR (1782)

THIS SECTION OF THE BOOK might be called the Natural History of the Smooth Deal. It is concerned with the ecology of our politics—the environmental factors that condition and shape both parties and voters. If any theme predominates, it is the curious way that traditional problems have become their opposites. The irony of American civilization is that in so many respects it has succeeded too well. There is no better illustration of this than the manner in which the melting pot has turned into a pressure cooker.

II

With scarcely a murmur of discussion, the Government recently put Ellis Island on the auction block. It had become an anachronism, and the Bureau of the Budget saw a chance to save a few pennies by selling this superfluous real estate. One bidder wanted to convert the island into an amusement park, and others proposed study centers and training schools. Although the fate of Ellis Island by now may be settled, I would propose a museum. The purpose would be to commemorate the contribution of the immigrant to the vigor of American life. The first exhibit would not be the Pilgrims—those worthy pioneers deserve a rest—but instead Tom Paine, the British alien who was the first to demand American independence. After Paine, another group of foreign-born citizens would be included, all purposeful malcontents and men of generous vision: Alexander Hamilton (West Indies), Albert Gallatin (Switzerland), Carl Schurz (Germany), Joseph Pulitzer (Hungary), Samuel Gompers (Great Britain), John Peter Altgeld (Germany), and Felix Frankfurter (Austria). Then, near the exit, a table would be set up at which visitors could write to Congress demanding a drastic liberalization of present immigration laws.

For as much as anything else, the streams of aliens who reached our shores have been the agents of constructive change. The discontent among the immigrants and their children has been one of the imperatives of our national progress. The case has been best stated by Arthur M. Schlesinger, Sr., in his *American as Reformer*:

> Early or late, these transplanted Europeans were men who rebelled against conditions as they found them in their homelands—against a class society, against religious and economic oppression—and unlike their more docile neighbors, they carried their rebellion to the point of going to a distant continent where life was strange, dangers abounded, and new careers must be sought. The departure

of such folk slowed down the impetus for change at home, just as it tended to quicken it in the adopted country.

From the days of Jefferson, Jackson, and Lincoln, the melting pot has been a source of political ferment. The struggles for suffrage, anti-slavery, trade unionism, coopera-tives, public education, and the eight-hour day—all of these are related to our immigrant experience. It is no accident that the New Deal coincided with the coming of age of the ethnic minorities who swarmed through Ellis Island decades before. It would be possible to examine in detail the history of states as diverse as New York, Rhode Island, and Wisconsin, and the careers of politicians as different as Fiorello LaGuardia, Frank J. Lausche, Jacob Javits, Robert M. La Follette, Sr., and Al Smith, to demonstrate the pervasive effect of the melting pot. But that would require a volume in itself; and I would prefer to make the safe generalization that one of the strengths of the American political system has been the mingling of Anglo-Saxon and European strains. Ours is a hybrid system, falling into no European category, a blend of individualism and collectiv-ism which reflects both the Yankee's distrust of government and the immigrant's reliance on government to broaden opportunity. What has kept us from becoming static has in great part been the successive waves of ethnic minorities who have used the ballot to creative ends.

No less important, the presence of the foreign-born has given a degree of variety to a country with a depressing surface uniformity. The aliens brought their songs, their theater, their art, their literature—Bach choirs, *Turnverein*, polkas, Swiss cheese, the delectable bagel. They also brought their newspapers. The *Zeitung*, the first foreign-language paper in America, was founded in 1732 by an enterprising Philadelphian, Benjamin Franklin. The New York *Staats-Zeitung*, which became a daily in 1848, soon claimed the largest German-language circulation in the world. In 1870, Milwaukee had five dailies in the German tongue, and only two in English. During the first decades of this century, Ayer's *Directory of Newspapers and Periodicals* listed some 1,000 publications in 36 languages, including Albanian, Arabic, Armenian, Carpatho-Russian, Chinese, Czech, Estonian, Finnish, Korean, Ukranian, Welsh, Yiddish—and one in Cherokee. Could any other nation in the world boast so multifarious a press?

III

But all this has swiftly faded. Between 1940 and 1949, a third of the existing foreign press passed away; Ayer's lists only 498 publications in a foreign tongue for 1960, and the total is inexorably declining. Milwaukee, a city which once posted "English Spoken Here" signs in store windows, now is served by a bi-weekly in the German language. We have all become Americans now—with a vengeance.

The process has been hastened by a counter-tendency which can be traced to the melting pot. If the foreign-born were agents for change, their presence also set in motion the nativist movement. The entire vocabulary of "un-Americanism" and "loyalty" springs from our experience as a Nation of Nations and Mother of Exiles. In Great Britain or France, where nationality is taken for granted, it would be unthinkable for the national legislature to appoint a standing committee to investigate "un-British" or "un-French" ideas. The notion of un-Americanism presupposes a stereotype to which the foreign-born should conform; all too often, they have.

Distrust of the alien was evident as early as the 1790's, when the Alien and Sedition Act (the coupling of terms is suggestive) was aimed at "Gallic" extremists who took democracy too seriously. Harrison Gray Otis, a spokesman of the nativists, declared that he "did not wish to invite hordes of wild Irishmen, nor the turbulent and disorderly of all parts of the world, to come here with the view to disturb our tranquility. . . ." At about this time, the word "Americanism" was coined by the Reverend John Witherspoon, himself a Scotch immigrant. Witherspoon, however, used the word in a linguistic sense; the term soon acquired a different connotation.

Hordes of turbulent aliens continued to fill the steerage of ships bound for the New World. More often than not, they had a less than reverent attitude to the status quo. In reaction, a Native American Association was founded in 1837, and this became the genesis of the American (Know-Nothing) Party of the 1850's. Speaking of the aliens, Henry Davis Winters warned in 1855: "They aspire to play reformers; and insolently form associations and devise plans to improve our homely American liberty into the likeness of the bloody and drunken dream of French and German liberty." Other horrors were depicted by Frederick Rinehart Anspach: ". . . It is not from Catholics alone that the danger is to be apprehended, but socialists and infidels. . . . They are impatient to abolish every sabbath law, consume every sanctuary, break every marriage tie, and turn this land into a brothel and pandemonium."

Some decades later, an event occurred which seemed to confirm every nativist fantasy. During an anarchist-led demonstration in Chicago, a bomb exploded and seven persons were killed. Although their actual complicity in the Haymarket explosion of 1886 was not proved, six immigrants (five of them German) and one native-born American were hanged. The press outdid itself in denouncing the "scum and offal of Europe" and the "cutthroats of Beezlebub from the Rhine, the Danube, the Vistula, and the Elbe." Fittingly, the controversy produced a prototype of Senator McCarthy, one Captain Michael J. Schaack of the Chicago police, whose book, *Anarchy and the Anarchists* (1889), was the authentic forebear of thousands of tracts to come. Captain Schaack enjoyed the publicity. "He wanted bombs to be found there, here, all around, everywhere . . . ," Police Chief Frederick Ebersold later testified. "After we got the anarchist societies broken up, Schaack wanted to send out men to organize new societies right away. . . . He wanted to keep the thing boiling— keep himself prominent before the public." History does not record whether Captain Schaack carried a briefcase stuffed with documents.

But all this was a mild prelude to the passions aroused during World War I when a contagion of xenophobia seized the country. Sauerkraut was solemnly rebaptized "liberty cabbage," and the world made safer for democracy by banning Wagner from the opera stage. Then came the Bolshevik Revolution. Writing in *Forum* magazine, Lewis Allen Browne sputtered:

> Bolshevism in America is the excrescence of the political melting pot—the social refuse, or slag, that will not fuse— the impure or foreign substance in our population. . . . American Bolshevism is made of Germans, Austrians, Mexicans, East Indians, and paid hirelings—Americans not worthy of the name—Russians, fanatics and anarchists from everywhere, people from little provinces, Lithu-

anians, Swedes, Norwegians, Danes, Letts—all types, from thugs and the illiterate, to the erratic and exotic intellectuals.

It was in this mood that the campaign to halt immigration began after the war. On May 26, 1924, President Coolidge signed the country's most restrictive immigration act, which, in its essentials, remains the law of the land. To all purposes this has ended the immigrant "problem." In 1959, a trickle of 260,686 managed to wend through the restrictive clauses designed to preserve America from foreign taint.

IV

Now that it is over—now that we are all Americans—the obsessions of the past seem absurd. A descendant of the "wild hordes" of Irishmen now sits in the White House, and the Republic seems likely to survive. In this respect, surely, the various "assimilation" campaigns have been successful. The painful tensions between the Yankee and the immigrant have eased, and few will feel any nostalgia for the era when the Ku Klux Klan was able to veto the choice of Al Smith at a Democratic Convention, as the Klan did in 1924.

But in a larger sense, the victory of assimilation has entailed a national failure. The arrival of the immigrants held open the possibility of building a true plural society in which unity could be rooted in a larger degree of cultural diversity. There was the promise of building a new kind of society in which the interplay of different ethnic groups could be a continuing source of vitality.

We have chosen the way of a mass society. It is our national weakness, as Tocqueville long ago observed, to distrust difference and to seek the imposition of a uniform mode of life. Thus, the expression of dissent among the foreign-born was too often equated with disloyalty. Fifty years ago, Randolph Bourne detected the dangers inherent in the cult of Americanism:

> What we emphatically do not want is that these distinctive qualities should be washed out into a tasteless, colorless fluid of uniformity. Already we have far too much of this insipidity—masses of people who are cultural half-breeds, neither assimilated Anglo-Saxons nor nationals of another culture. . . . Our cities are filled with these half-breeds who retain their foreign names but have lost the foreign savor. This does not mean that . . . they have been really Americanized. It means that, letting slip from whatever native culture that they had, they have substituted for it only the most rudimentary American—the American culture of the cheap newspaper, the movies, the popular song, the ubiquitous automobile. . . . Just as surely as we tend to disintegrate these nuclei of nationalistic culture do we tend to create hordes of men and women without a spiritual country, cultural outlaws without taste, without standards but those of the mob.

Though Kennedy may sit in the White House, in a sense the Ku Klux Klan has won. The obsessions of the past may seem silly, but we are still their prisoner. Few nations on earth demand so many public professions of loyalty, in the form of oaths and vows, as does the United States. The insistence on adherence to a single standard of Americanism has helped to produce a situation in which all our politicians seem to look alike. And the strongest nation on earth is still so frightened of foreigners that its immigration laws make it nearly as inaccessible as the icy Antarctic. That museum on Ellis Island might do some good.

10 /

The Twilight of Regionalism

> The time . . . is anticipated when the language,
> manners, customs, political and religious sentiments of
> the mixed mass of the people who inhabit the United
> States, shall have become so assimilated, as that all nominal
> distinctions shall be lost in the general and honourable
> name of Americans.
>
> —JEDIDIAH MORSE, *The American Geography* (1789)

THE TIME ANTICIPATED by the worthy Reverend
Morse, a Congregationalist pastor in Charleston, Massachusetts, has very nearly come. But the divine works in
mysterious ways, and Reverend Morse might have been
surprised that His design has been given an assist by Jack
Paar, Coca-Cola, and the worldly slick publications.

It is of course true that in the strictest sense regional
differences (always with the exception of the South) have
not been strong in the United States. Lord Bryce observed
as much in *The American Commonwealth*. If you were
to talk to a hundred persons at a British political convention, Bryce suggested, "you would be struck by more
diversity between the notions and tastes and mental habits
of the individuals comprising that one hundred than if

you tried the same experiment with a hundred Americans . . . similarly gathered in a convention from every state in the Union."

Still, though Americans may tend to look alike and talk alike, in matters political they certainly have not behaved alike. At a British political convention, one imagines, habits of decorum bring parliamentary order and a surface civility to an assemblage of Scotsmen, Welshmen, and Englishmen. This is not true of American political conventions, which in years past often went to an opposite extreme, resembling feeding time in the monkey house.

Even the Republicans were once far from being a Bland Old Party. When Lincoln was elected in 1860, Congressman Horace C. Maynard of Tennessee called shocked attention to the "dapple hue" of the party that was about to take office. "I beseech you, gentlemen," pleaded Maynard, "to look at your own party . . . and see of what heterogeneous elements it is composed":

> Old Whigs and old Democrats; followers of Thomas Jefferson; admirers of Alexander Hamilton; friends of Jackson, friends of Clay; masons, anti-masons; "barnburners," "hunkers," "renters," "anti-renters"; "woolyheads," "silver grays"; Know-nothings, Americans, foreigners, Catholics; protective tariff men, free trade men, bullion men; radicals, conservatives; men of strict construction, and men of no construction; men of unquestionable honesty, and men whose honesty I will not venture to call into question; men of all grades of political sentiment, all shades of political opinion, all bedded together, heads and heels, covered by a single blanket, and that woven of African wool.

Congressman Maynard, of course, was not trying to be "objective." Neither was Walt Whitman, a loyal Lincoln

man, when he turned his pen on the strange mixture that
turned up at Democratic conventions in exactly the same
period:

> . . . the meanest kind of . . . blowing officer-holders,
> office seekers . . . malignants, conspirators, murderers,
> fancy-men, custom-house clerks, contractors, kept editors,
> spaniels well trained to carry and fetch, jobbers, infidels,
> disunionists, terrorists, mail-riflers, slave-catchers, pushers
> of slavery, creatures of the President, spies, bribers, com-
> promisers, lobbyers, spongers, ruined sports, expelled gam-
> blers, policy backers, monte-dealers, duellists, carriers of
> concealed weapons, deaf men, pimpled men, scarred in-
> side with vile disease, gaudy outside with gold chains
> made from the people's money; crawling, serpentine men;
> the lousy combings and born freedom-sellers of the earth.

Those who watched the two political conventions could
see nothing like this in 1960. *Maverick* was on another
channel; the delegates were well-behaved folk who had
gathered, almost in a *pro forma* way, to ratify the selection
of candidates with a minimum of fuss. The Democrats
were surprisingly passive, and the Republicans were so
many sheep in sheep's clothing. Only in the Texas delegation did a little static arise on the nomination of Mr.
Nixon. What, indeed, would the country do without
Texas?

II

But the winds of change can be detected even in Texas.
In 1932, the Lone Star candidate for the Presidency was
"Cactus Jack" Garner of Uvalde, whom John L. Lewis
upbraided as a "labor-baiting, poker-playing, whisky-
drinking, evil old man." But in 1960, the bands were

playing for Lyndon B. Johnson, whose nickname is a business-like LBJ and who is famed as the Capitol's slickest engineer of consent. Texas, along with the rest of the country, has come a long way from the time of "Pa" and "Ma" Ferguson (who took turns being Governor, thus proving that bedfellows can make strange politics).

The Senate these days is a less colorful citadel. Georgia's Herman Talmadge is reputedly the last of the tobacco chewers; the chamber's shiny brass cuspidor once brimmed with use. With the death of North Carolina's Clyde Hoey in 1954, the string tie and frock coat passed from the cloakroom. Tom Connally of Texas, who is remembered for his virile profanity, was the last to sport a duck-tailed, curl-fringed haircut. Once upon a time, "Pitchfork Ben" Tillman of South Carolina threatened to disembowel the President with a pitchfork. Such blasphemies are not heard on *Meet the Press*, where even James O. Eastland, pride of Mississippi, sounds like a Rhodes Scholar in comparison to Claghorns past.

Industrialism, urban culture, and especially television have had a profound effect on the New South. The rednecks and wool-hats can counter the NAACP with a few lynchings, they can show up the Supreme Court by spitting at a few schoolgirls—but what can they do about NBC? Arthur Godfrey and Ed Sullivan probably have a greater effect on racial mores than all the bayonets of the Union army. It is stretching only a little to say that we have become one nation, indivisible, under General Sarnoff.

On the pervasive effect of television, the expert testimony of Leonard Hall, former Republican National Chairman, warrants attention:

It is no exaggeration to say that television has wrought a

revolution in the country's political life. There is a story that they tell about Maine, for instance, that explains my point. Maine always was a Republican state. People were born Republicans, so they went to the polls and voted Republican. Then, suddenly, they voted for some Democrats up there—too many, from my viewpoint. So one day I asked an old Maine man what happened in his state. "Well," he said, "we can't do anything with this television. Our children were brought up to think that Democrats had horns. Now they see them on television and realize some of them don't have horns a-tall!"

As Mr. Hall suggests, the ubiquity of television has had a good deal to do with the decline of the one-party state. Consider the implications of the following table:

ONE-PARTY DELEGATIONS IN CONGRESS, 1942-1960

Year	Total of one-party states
1942	24
1944	23
1946	23
1948	21
1950	21
1952	19
1954	17
1956	14
1958	11
1960	12

Assuredly, it is no accident that the number of one-party fiefdoms falls off sharply after 1952, when television had become an important part of the political process. Voters were able to see that spokesmen of the underdog party really didn't have horns a-tall (or at least none that could not be hidden by the makeup man). In creating a two-party electorate, television has gone far toward bringing about real competition between the parties through most of the land.

III

To the extent that our cultural mixmaster has fostered racial enlightenment and encouraged party competition, the television industry is entitled to congratulate itself. But there are side effects that are far less desirable—both cultural and political. There are elements of diversity in our society well worth preserving which also seem doomed by NBC.

Take the matter of language. Frederic Cassidy of the University of Wisconsin, a dialect collector, is one of the scholars who is in a race with the juke box. "As usual most informants are elderly people who will not be with us much longer," Professor Cassidy remarked in one dialect study published in 1958, adding with scholarly pique, "—it makes one nearly desperate, the thought of how much is sure to be irrevocably lost."

Among the local usages that Professor Cassidy places on the casualty list are *pond-horse, scrapple, clabber milk, hushpuppies* (foods), *an open and shut day, it's spitting, raining pitchforks and hoe handles, squaw winter* (weather lore), and *hex, witching-stick, poky spot* (superstition). In Wisconsin alone, Dr. Cassidy found nine names for one children's game which consists of throwing a stick into the air and hitting it with another stick: *jap-stick, jippy-stick, nick-nock, cricket, peeny, whip stick, tip cat, minnow,* and *bat-the-stick.*

Across the country little rock pools have eluded the tides of national custom. The Eastern Shore of Maryland has its distinct archaic dialect, the fishermen on the coast of North Carolina speak in Devonshire accents that go back to the time of Sir Walter Raleigh, and in the Kentucky Hills, students of folk-lore have encountered authentic Elizabethan ballads. But the time is short; the rock pools are being washed away. Jesse Stuart, a Kentucky writer, remarked in sorrow of his mountaineer neighbors in 1957: "There isn't any dialect left with our youngsters. Only a few people of our older generation speak with any dialect. Even the nice idioms of our strong hill language are disappearing. If there are any ballads left among us, they should be gathered now."

It is true that regional distinctions have not been strong or persistent in the United States. Nevertheless, a regional culture once did flourish in New England, and traces of its heritage can be detected in the career of John F. Kennedy. And the South, in its final agony, is undergoing a literary renaissance. In a country too preoccupied with the present, the South's obsession with the past has been a source of creative strength. The town of Greenville, Mississippi has (according to the London *Times*) seventeen authors in print. What comparable Northern town would even bother to count?

IV

As with language, so with politics. The powerful state politician is being washed down the same drain as the jippy-stick and poky spot. It became a cliché during the 1960 campaign to observe that the Governor's chair was a death seat, and that the ambitious politician was now looking to the Senate as a forum. Local politics have lost much of their appeal as the eye of television makes

Washington seem closer to the living room than the state capital.

It could well be that in the end this nationalizing process will make an empty shell of the Federal system. The Founding Fathers valued a plural society and deliberately composed a Federal charter which would encourage the play of local factions. But the Fathers did not visualize the extra-constitutional innovation of television, which crosses state lines with an ease that would have dismayed Calhoun.

Those who regard the theory of state's rights as a mask for privilege—which it very often has been—may not mourn the passing of localism. But there is a good deal to be said for the Federal system in a country as big as the United States. Within the boundaries of a smaller political unit, a La Follette as well as a Faubus can find scope for his talent. New ideas can be tested, and publicized, as they were in Wisconsin, where the first unemployment insurance and workmen's compensation laws were put into effect. "Wisconsin," Theodore Roosevelt said in 1912, "has literally become a laboratory for wise experimental legislation."

During the 1930's, when it appeared that Upton Sinclair might become Governor of California on a radical platform known as EPIC (End Poverty in California), some Democrats were appalled. "Perhaps they'll get EPIC in California," came the sane reply of Franklin Delano Roosevelt.

What difference, I ask you, would that make in Duchess County, New York or Lincoln County, Maine? The beauty of our state-Federal system is that the people can experiment. If it has fatal consequences in one place, it has little effect upon the rest of the country. If a new, apparently fanatical, program works well, it will be copied. If it doesn't, you won't hear of it again.

But in the end, the use of the states as experimental stations depends on the degree of importance attached to local politics. The presence of four one-time Senators on the national tickets of the two major parties does not argue favorably for the future of state politics. The drift of events lends some substance to the fears that the nationalizing process has gone too far and that an ever more centralized government will be ruling an increasingly uniform populace. It may be an open and shut day in Washington, but in the provinces it is raining pitchforks and hoe handles.

11 /

The Old in Heart

> The college, we discovered, was muggy with modest
> ambitions; the little dreams were not of wealth or fame or
> monumental accomplishments, but of bureaucrats'
> offices in government and the corporations.
>
> —OSCAR HANDLIN (1951)

WHAT WOULD FRANCIS BACON make of the new
generation of Americans? In his essay on youth, Bacon
stressed that young men "stir more than they can quiet; fly
to the end without consideration of means and degrees;
pursue some principles which they have chanced upon
absurdly . . . use extreme remedies at first; and that which
doubleth all errors, will not acknowledge or retract them;
like an unready horse, that will neither stop nor turn."

The words sound odd in reference to a young generation
variously described as cool, beat, and silent. No, it is not
Bacon's description of youth, but rather of age that seems
applicable: "Men of age object too much, consult too
long, adventure too little, repent too soon, and seldom
drive business home to the full period, but content themselves with a mediocrity of success." It is this curious

reversal, so widely remarked and deplored, that accounts for the fascination among adults with two new prototypes of youthful dissent: William F. Buckley, Jr., and Jack Kerouac. During the Eisenhower years, these were the young men who seemed to pursue some principle which they had chanced upon absurdly. The neatly attired author of *God and Man at Yale* and the unbathed author of *On the Road* were greeted almost with yelps of delight by those who were looking for a sign of revolt among the young.

But was it revolt? Or were the Buckleyites and Beatniks the extreme expression of over-conformity during the Eisenhower years? On closer examination, there is good evidence that this was the case, and that the followers of Mr. Buckley and Mr. Kerouac have more in common than either group would care to acknowledge. Indeed, the consensus on vital points between the two groups, so outwardly unlike, is sufficiently striking to raise the question whether the word Buckbeat might not be the suitable generic term to describe both the reefer-smoking Dharma bums and the Ivy Leaguers who flocked to the "Youth for Goldwater" cause.

II

To begin with, the calm that has descended on the campus is surely not surprising. The present generation has grown up *with*—and not for or against—the New Deal, and therefore the old slogans have little meaning. International problems are far more ambiguous and cannot be fit into facile slogans. Most important, we live in a full-employment economy, and the transition from college to "real" life is so smooth as to be almost nonexistent for those youngsters who are looking for a snug berth in the business world.

Appropriately, the first report on how "different" the young had become appeared in the glossy pages of *Fortune*. In a survey of the class of '49, the magazine commented:

> It is what they don't want rather than what they do that the men of '49 know best. And what they don't want is risk. . . . They seem, to a stranger from another generation, somehow curiously old before their time. Above everything else, security has become their goal. . . . The class of '49 wants to work for somebody else—preferably somebody big.

Some 3,000 businesses were already recruiting on the campus in 1949. Four years later, virtually every firm worth the attention of Dun and Bradstreet was doing it. Colleges have come to stress vocational courses more than ever before, and to make things still easier, corporations have set up costly postgraduate training courses to ease the youngster into his new life. "The union between the world of organization and the college has been so cemented," writes William H. Whyte, Jr., in *The Organization Man*, "that today's seniors can see a continuity between the college and the life thereafter that we never did. Come graduation, they do not go outside into a hostile world; they transfer."

Students so fortunately situated would be foolish to question the status quo. And the new generation is notable for its lack of foolishness, and this includes not only the business-minded but also the putative intellectuals. No other generation, Wallace Markfield remarks in a symposium in *The New Leader*, "has pursued the Good Job so wisely and so well. . . . To their lot fall the foundation plums, the berths with the better magazines and book-houses, the research sinecures. They are almost never un-employed; they are only between grants." In view of this languor on the campus, it is understandable that William F. Buckley, Jr., has aroused such sympathetic attention.

I I I

When he was fifteen, William F. Buckley was urged by his father to "learn to be more moderate in the expression of your views and try to express them in a way that would give as little offense as possible." We can be grateful that young Buckley ignored this parental nudge. Although his background is very much like that of President Kennedy (Buckley has three brothers, six sisters, and is the son of a self-made millionaire of Irish stock), Mr. Buckley has found moderation in any form distasteful.

But only in his dogmatism does he resemble his fore-bears on the campus. Campus rebels used to accuse college administrations of servility to big business; Buckley reversed the formula and accused Yale of persuading its students to be "atheistic socialists."* The older breed tended to identify with the far left, but Buckley championed McCarthyism ("a movement around which men of good will and stern morality may close ranks"). He and his followers have given sympathetic support to the most

---

* This charge was elaborated in *God and Man at Yale*, a true *tour de force*. It names (by my count) nine faculty members as overt atheists or collectivists. Since at the time Yale had a faculty of 1,214, this suggested that .007 per cent of the teaching staff was successfully Bolshevizing the cream of Choate and Groton. Even Lenin would be impressed.

hopeless causes, ranging from elimination of the income tax to the restoration of Archduke Otto to his throne in Vienna. It is fortunate that Yale was unable to convert a man of Buckley's zeal to the "other" side.

Mr. Buckley has the special appeal of a man with a cause in a generation that hardly seems to know what the word means. His example has been contagious. A flock of little Buckleys now torment social scientists in colleges large and small. By the end of the 1950's, the "revolt on the right" had achieved somewhat the same position in campus politics as the old leftist movement. The new sect's chief organ, *The National Review*, resembles *The Nation* and *The New Republic* in format, and the Intercollegiate Society of Individualists (founded in 1953) was consciously patterned on the Intercollegiate Socialist Society of years past. ISI has since been joined by YFG (Youth for Goldwater), NSCFTLO (National Student Committee for the Loyalty Oath), and YAFF (Young Americans for Freedom). These are the initials that now provoke controversy—not AYD, YPSL, SLID, SDA, YCL, LYL.* And, in a familiar pattern, the YAFFites have infiltrated the Young Republicans, purging the hopelessly liberal Nixon partisans and turning the YGOP into a front for Goldwater.

This shift in position reflects a broader tendency on the campus. During the 1920's and 1930's, the academic

---

* These obscure glyphs stand for American Youth for Democracy, Young Peoples Socialist League, Student League for Industrial Democracy, Students for Democratic Action, Young Communist League, and Labor Youth League. To my knowledge, only the YPLSs and SDA are still active. The SDA is affiliated with Americans for Democratic Action and sometimes (it is a pleasure to report) annoys the nestors of ADA with proposals that are "unrealistic."

hierarchy was part of the conservative Establishment, but in the post-war years a liberal consensus came to pre-dominate—while precisely the reverse tendency was at work among the students. Thus in 1952 and 1956, the faculty of Princeton University gave a majority vote to Stevenson, but the students were overwhelmingly for Eisenhower. The switch in position creates a new opportunity for campus rebels. As Dwight Macdonald was the first to observe, "The line Buckley has taken permits him to enjoy the pleasures of unorthodox rebellion (within Yale), and of conformity (outside Yale)." The rebels of the right are more prudent than their predecessors; they can raise a stink about Dewey (John or Tom) and yet pass into the business world unscathed. Even the fiercest YAFFmen, we may be sure, will not be blackballed by General Motors.

IV

However, we do worse than hire our heretics: we institutionalize them. As Dan Wakefield notes in a profile of Mr. Buckley, the extremist today becomes incorporated into the public rituals of the society he attacks. "In a sense," Mr. Wakefield writes,

> the process Buckley has undergone is similar to the experience of Jack Kerouac—first attacked by the majority voices of the society he is criticizing; then, after more books offering the same violent criticism come forth, the rebel is treated with increasing "tolerance," detachment, even wry amusement and patronizing camaraderie; and increasingly, the rebel becomes a favorite performer before audiences who wholly disagree with what he says, but would defend to the death his right to entertain them

by saying it—and the louder he says it the louder they applaud.

This is what has happened to the Beatniks, the first Bohemians to be nationally merchandised. The process was swift. In November, 1952, John Clellon Holmes used the phrase "beat generation" for the first time in print in *The New York Times Magazine,* crediting its coinage to another young novelist, Jack Kerouac. The phrase didn't catch until five years later when Mr. Kerouac published *On the Road*—and before you could say Arthur Hays Sulzburger even *The New York Times* was praising Mr. Kerouac as a latter-day Hemingway.

Earlier generations of rebels could complain of inattention by the bourgeois press, but the Beatniks were smothered in clippings. Jeers turned into appreciative chuckles as the Beats ceased being artists and became performers. In San Francisco, the movement's home office, tourists began demanding to see beards and sandals, and Beatnik kits were soon available to locals who might want to oblige. Between the toothpaste and perfume counter at the drug store, you could find scores of paperbacks by the Beats, and many seemed to have the photograph of the same pad and dark-haired chick on the cover. Soon, no college symposium was complete without a hipster who would upbraid the audience and perhaps disrobe on the rostrum for an encore. One began to have the uneasy feeling that if the Beatniks had not existed, *Time-Life* would have invented them.

Still, to those who value a little discord for its own sake, the Beats were something. Amid a generation that was prematurely conventional, the Beatniks showed that there were other paths to success than the one lined with retirement plans. They may have been, as one Britisher called them, "Nihilism's Organization Men," but nevertheless there was a faint trace of nihilism.

There is a good reason why both Buckley and Kerouac have found an indulgent audience. In a sense, the ideas of both are caricatures of widely held American beliefs. Both YAFFites and Beatniks champion an essentially egoistic attitude to life, in the philosophic sense of the term. Both elevate the person over the community and see the purpose of society as the satisfaction of individual desires—whether through puffing reefers or accumulating property without taxes. Both movements are devoid of social vision and display a profound distrust for any collective enterprise, including the universities that both colonize. ("I would rather be governed by the first 2,000 people in the telephone directory than by the Harvard University faculty," Mr. Buckley has said—though it looks as if his worst fear is being realized.)

In the case of the Beats, this egoism is orgiastic, filled with suggestions of dope, sexual athletics, and mystic visions. "We're no action group, man," one hipster informed Eugene Burdick, ". . . I stay cool, far out, alone. When I flip it's over something I feel, only me. That big ole group out there who want you to be buck private, bell-boy, neat college boy, Brooks, MG driving, sick and money hungry. Me, I get my kicks where I can. *They* . . . I don't care what they do, O.K.?" Norman Podhoretz, in an incisive study of the Beats, points out that Mr. Kerouac's conception of feeling "is one that only a solipsist could believe in—and a solipsist, be it noted, is a man who does not relate to anything outside himself."

If Kerouac's followers are emotional solipsists, Buckley's are economic solipsists. *The Individualist*, organ of the ISI, is crowded with eloquent statements on "the right of the individual to an inviolable area of freedom." Here, there is verbal unanimity between Beatniks and YAFFmen; John Clellon Holmes, in an essay entitled "The Philosophy of the Beat Generation," stresses that to the hipster "the foundation of all systems, moral or social, is the indestructible unit of the single individual."

But the difference is that Buckley's individualism is invariably discussed in economic terms; ISI has scheduled no protest march on NBC, which has been offering individualists a choice between private eyes, westerns, and crooked quiz shows. Moreover, a sonorous liturgy is invoked to justify the individual's supremacy over society—the prose is more George Sokolsky than Henry Miller. The founding statement of Young Americans for Freedom, which has been endorsed, *ex cathedra*, by Mr. Buckley, proclaims "that foremost among the transcendent values is the individual's use of his God-given free will, whence derives his right to be free from the restrictions of arbitrary force."

Then, after an epiphany of "thats," we literally get down to business:

> That when government interferes with the work of the market economy, it tends to reduce the moral and physical strength of the nation; that when it takes from one man to bestow on another, it diminishes the incentive of the first, the integrity of the second, and the moral autonomy of both.

Translated from YAFFese, this seems to mean that income taxes, Social Security, and welfare legislation are downright immoral.

In any event, this was the form that youthful insurgency took during the Eisenhower years. There are signs of change as the Kennedy era begins, notably in the warm response on the campus to the newly-formed Peace Corps. It may well be that the Buckbeats were a passing phenomenon, a measure of a time when the repudiation of community had gone so far that even intelligent young men could seriously argue that the highest purpose of society was to make each citizen a little world unto himself.

12 /

Bohemia Moves Uptown

> Of all the enemies of literature, success is the
> most insidious.
>
> —CYRIL CONNOLLY

TIMES *have* CHANGED. We now have a First Lady
who, in response to a questionnaire, selected Baudelaire,
Oscar Wilde, and Diaghilev as the three eminent men of
the past she would like to meet. The tastes of Jacqueline
Bouvier Kennedy are the most obvious sign of the new
status of the artist and writer in American life. The mind
boggles at the thought of previous First Ladies inviting
a Baudelaire or an Oscar Wilde to dine at the White
House—but in the Kennedy era, the idea is not so far-
fetched. Indeed, within a month after moving to the
White House, Mrs. Kennedy broke tea-biscuits with e. e.
cummings.

Bohemia has come a long way in America from the
days when Mabel Dodge's salon in Greenwich Village
raised eyebrows because such scandalous ideas as birth-
control and psychoanalysis were discussed in mixed company. To be precise, Bohemia has moved Uptown. In

1912, the year that Mabel Dodge opened her doors to guests ranging from John Reed, Walter Lippmann (then a Socialist), and Bill Haywood, the burly IWW leader— in that year, a chasm seemed to divide Uptown from Downtown. Geographically, Uptown was the area above Fourteenth Street; intellectually, Uptown was the world of stuffy orthodoxy. This was the year that Max Eastman received a note reading, "You are elected editor of the *Masses*. No pay." The same year, the *Titanic* sank, Theodore Roosevelt bolted the Republican Party, Eugene Debs received nearly a million votes, and Edna St. Vincent Millay, only nineteen, wrote *Renascence*. The mood of the time was expressed by John Reed in a book of doggerel dedicated in 1912 to Lincoln Steffens; one passage of A *Day in Bohemia* read:

> Yet we are free who live in Washington Square,
> We dare to think as Uptown wouldn't dare.

Reed's boast sounds quaint today. Chances are that had John Reed lived, he would have become an Uptown Bohemian, too—a roving editor for *Look* and a regular guest on "Open End." His most insurrectionary activity, if he still lived in the Village, would probably be to help the middle-class agrarian reformers overthrow Carmine De Sapio and his Tammany proletariat.

I I

The most obvious example of Bohemia's triumph is painting. It is instructive to glance at the old telephone directories in the Library of Congress. The Manhattan directory of 1924 lists only one art gallery, but four years later the category was no longer so novel: 86 were listed.

By 1944, there were 270 galleries, and in 1960 the total was up to 483. Thus the *avant-garde* has moved from the *Yellow Book* to the yellow pages, and it was not long before *Fortune* was reminding its readers that modern art was a gilt-edged investment.

It did not seem so gilt-edged in 1913, when Manhattan's 69th Infantry Regiment Armory was adorned with no less than 1,600 paintings, drawings, and sculpture. This was the Armory Exhibition which first introduced the modernist movement to America—the cubists, *Fauves*, post-impressionists, and the Ashcan School. Uptown was horrified and fascinated. "The Armory show is *pathological!* It is hideous!" said *The New York Times*. Royal Cortissoz, critic of *The New York Herald*, called it "unadulterated cheek," adding, in a familiar refrain: "The United States is invaded by aliens, thousands of whom constitute so many acute perils to the health of the body politic. Modernism is of precisely the same heterogeneous alien origin and is imperiling the republic of art in the same way." Thus were Picasso, Matisse, Van Gogh, Gauguin, Braque, and Roualt first received.

But not all Uptown reactions were hostile. Theodore Roosevelt, for one, though he was critical of "extremists," was frankly sympathetic to the idea of innovation. Museum directors were interested, and elsewhere, in the words of Thomas Craven,

> an inspiring burst of vitality shot forth. Galleries devoted exclusively to the modern idiom were founded; eccentric magazines, containing hateful manifestos and bewildering illustrations, were born overnight; and Greenwich Village emerged as the locale of the new movement, the Bohemia where starving painters, the addled and sincere together with charlatans, subsisted. . . .

Slowly but surely the modernists advanced. In 1928, a new outpost was founded when the Museum of Modern Art opened its doors in an office building with an exhibit of French painters who had been represented in the Armory show. Shortly, the Museum moved to new quarters on West Fifty-Third Street, and its clientele became steadily more chic. In time, the Museum became as respectable as the Chase National Bank, and the worth of its stock just as secure. Speaking of the Museum, Russell Lynes remarks that in its early days it was run by

> young men in their twenties and thirties, full of ardor, eager to experiment, and engaged in a battle that was almost exclusively theirs to fight. In many respects their battle has been won. Now the men who run it are in their fifties, the little outpost has become an established, wealthy, and elaborately organized institution and a vested interest. . . .

Surely it was a symbol of Bohemia's ultimate victory that today the Governor of New York—a Rockefeller, no less—is the Museum's proudest patron. The circle was closed after World War II when the Whitney Museum of American Art moved from its old quarters in Greenwich Village to a new site next to the Museum of Modern Art, bringing two major collections within lunching distance of Madison Avenue.

III

The typewriter followed the paint-pot, as the Village's ephemeral magazines also became established and elaborately organized institutions. This can best be seen by examining the reincarnation of the *Masses* and the *Little Review* in more respectable Uptown guise.

Under the editorship of Max Eastman, the *Masses* was the Village's brashest voice. John Reed drafted the statement of purposes which animated the magazine during its great days:

> The broad purpose of the *Masses* is a social one; to everlastingly attack old systems, old morals, old prejudices—the whole weight of outworn thought that dead men have saddled upon us. . . . We intend to be arrogant, impertinent, in bad taste, but not vulgar. We will be bound by no creed, but will express them all, providing they be radical.

Thus the *Masses* became the vehicle through which Bohemia hooted at the manners and morals of Uptown. Eastman devised the one-line caption to give more impudent impact to illustrations contributed by John Sloan, Art Young, George Bellows, Boardman Robinson, Stuart Davis, and Robert Minor. The poems and articles were equal parts burlesque and polemic, and bourgeois tastes—no less than bourgeois politics—were the target of the *Masses*.

But during World War I, hooting went out of fashion, and the magazine ran afoul of the Government for exercising its right of free speech too strenuously. In 1917, the *Masses* expired—but its spirit survived. Eight years later, Harold Ross founded an Uptown edition which in its handling of cartoons and satiric tone owed a clear debt to its more radical cousin. The best authority on the transition is the distinguished artist, John Sloan: "The *Masses* set a pace and had an influence of all periodicals after [it]. Certainly the *New Yorker*, in a more sophisticated and less liberal way, patterned itself on the early *Masses*."

The *Masses* wound up in suburbia; the *Little Review* was given an academic gown. Founded in 1914 by Margaret Anderson, the *Little Review* was emblazoned by the work of an exceptional group, including T. S. Eliot, Ezra Pound, William Carlos Williams, and Ernest Hemingway. Its most luminous achievement was the first publication, in installments, of Joyce's *Ulysses*. "It was the supreme moment of the epoch," according to Miss Anderson: according to the Society for the Suppression of Vice, it was smut. But despite continued harassment, the *Little Review* continued to chronicle Bloomsday for three years. No less than four issues of the magazine, Allen Churchill writes in *The Improper Bohemian*, "were BURNED."

In time the little magazine became less flammable. The *Little Review* (which lasted until 1929), and its countless cousins elsewhere with names like *Secession, Broom, Fugitive*, and *transition* gave way to a new kind of review endowed by universities and foundations (and in one case, by the Aga Khan). Rather than publish experimental writing, the characteristic review (*Kenyon, Sewanee, Hudson*, and *Western*) now devotes most of its pages to critical articles freighted with the smell of Ph.D. "The little magazines of the 1920's really deserved the name," Malcolm Cowley remarks. "They were smaller in size, smaller in circulation, shorter lived . . . they were usually edited by very young men, and their tone was informal, even irresponsible."

Two further quotations are pertinent. The first is from William Barrett, a former editor of *Partisan Review*, and is harsh: "With the tightening up all along the line in our national life during the decade past, the literary reviews have become invaded more and more by the spirit of the museum; instead of struggling to keep things open and alive, they are engaged in enshrining the dead."

The second is from Secretary of State Dean Rusk, and is broadly symptomatic. According to Dwight Macdonald, when Mr. Rusk was president of the Rockefeller Foundation, he was worried about the dispiriting effect of perpetual subsidies on little magazines—perhaps he had been reading a few. "Do you think it would make them soft," he asked a visitor, "if they knew where their next subsidy was coming from?" No doubt a foundation-financed interdisciplinary, intercollegiate, and intergalactic study group is pondering the matter now.

I V

But it is not only the benevolence of foundations and Uptown's hospitality to modernism that has brought the intellectual closer to his society. In politics, the old socialist faith has been shaken—or better, annihilated—by disillusionment with Stalinism, the Moscow trials, and, in a different way, with the realization of the welfare state. Moreover, the chasm between the poor and the rich in the United States has been closed to the point where poverty is not a major national problem.

The result is that the highbrow has become pretty much like everybody else in the middle-class world. His aesthetic sensibilities may be more cultivated, and he may be horrified by mass culture—but his old enemies of the Academy have been routed and the champions of modernism (Joyce, Picasso, Stravinsky, etc.) are regularly glorified in *Life*. Politically, the intellectual is now an egghead—a longhair shorn of his locks. Rather than Utopia, he will settle for Stevenson or Kennedy, if he is interested in politics at all.

Many are not; Dwight Macdonald, a one-time anarchist and Trotskyite, speaks for a group so large that he may become uncomfortable:

> The questions that now interest me are not the "big" ones: What To Do About Russia? Is Planning Incompatible With Capitalism? Will There Be a Depression? Does America Need a Labor Party or a Revitalized Democratic Party—or Just a Dozen More TVA's? Is World Government the Answer to the H-Bomb? These seem to me either unimportant or unanswerable. . . . It is the "small" questions that now seem to me significant. What is a good life? How do we know what's good and what's bad? . . . Who am I? How can I live lovingly, truthfully, pleasurably?

All this is well and good; the Uptown Bohemians are surely less doctrinaire and less strident. Their material lot has emphatically improved, and their status has probably risen to a rank slightly above the chiropractor and below the banker. But it is worth asking two questions: (1) How productive has Bohemia been in its Uptown environment? (2) Assuming that success has been good for the artist, has it also been good for society?

Concerning the first question, the answer all too frequently is statistical. The litany is familiar and comforting. In 1920, there were about 100 symphony orchestras in the United States; by 1959, the total was 1,142. Classical record sales now account for 35 to 40 per cent of the industry's total business—as against 15 per cent in 1946. The number of FM-only stations (a category which includes most Good Music stations) has grown from 57 in 1950 to 312 in 1960. In 1945, you could find only 112 book titles in paperback; fifteen years later, the racks were bulging with some 7,000 titles. There were only 12 art movie theaters in 1948, but by 1960 you could sip *espresso* and see Ingmar Bergman at 550 art cinemas.

These are impressive statistics, and they help the Voice of America to persuade foreigners that Culture is important in our country. But one has the uneasy feeling that *Pravda* could play the same game, *e.g.*, under the Soviet Union's Third Five-Year Plan, x million copies of Tolstoy were printed, y thousand ballets performed, and z hundred Good (or Better) Music Stations established. And no doubt Soviet architects have on the drawing board a temple of culture every bit as vast and ugly as the Lincoln Center. What this statistical game conceals is the fact that during the past decade Russia's only major contribution to world literature was written by a pariah whose roots were in pre-revolutionary culture.

In this respect, there is an uncomfortable parallel with our own country. Our leading figures tend to be critics and interpreters, not creators. In past decades, although there were no Fulbrights, no writers' conferences, no Lincoln Centers, we somehow managed to produce Hemingway, Fitzgerald, Dos Passos, Wolfe, Faulkner, O'Neill, and cummings. It is this cultural capital that largely supports the Uptown museum—the statistics really amount to attendance records. Possibly we are in the midst of one of those cycles of consolidation which our historians are always graphing. But it *does* seem a lamentably long cycle.

Moreover, there is an element of unwarranted self-congratulation in the cultural numbers game. Statistics can point both ways. In Great Britain, for example, more book titles are published each year than in the United States, despite the discrepancy in population—and, according to Dr. Gallup, the average American reads fewer books than the citizens of any other major democracy. There is also the matter of quality. You can buy anything from Mickey Spillane to Lionel Trilling in the drug store, but the magazine rack offers nothing comparable to the *Economist, New Statesman, Spectator,* or *Encounter.*

Finally, there is the broader question of whether the "democratization" of Bohemia has not actually resulted in devaluing high culture without a commensurate improvement in mass culture. We get our Stravinsky, but in candied form with a sugared commentary by Leonard Bernstein; we get what Dwight Macdonald calls Midcult, which "pretends to respect the standards of high culture while in fact it waters them down and vulgarizes them." In the end, there is a blurring of standards in which Herman Wouk and Herman Melville are lumped together as "important" novelists of the sea.

V

These objections, however, can be met by the argument that in the Cold War it is more important for the artist to be patriotic than productive, and that conflict between the intellectual and his society is somehow damaging to the image of America. This, roughly, seems to be the view of *Time* magazine. In a cover story on Jacques Barzun, entitled "America and the Intellectual: The Great Reconciliation," *Time* concluded that "in 1956, it would seem, the intellectual has ceased weeping. He is, in fact, closer than ever before to assuming the role he originally played in America as the critical but sympathetic—and wholly indispensable—bearer of America's message." As *Time* saw it, the "Man of Protest" had largely been supplanted by the "Man of Affirmation" as more intellectuals came to realize "that they are true and proud participants in the American dream."

Surely a little scepticism is in order. Translate *Time's* assertion into Russian, and you have exactly the complaint of the Soviet government concerning Boris Pasternak: that he was a "Man of Protest" and not a "Man of Affirmation." The Russian intellectual, admittedly, has far more to protest about, but the principle is the same. The All-Union Congress of Soviet Writers also insists that the proper role of the artist is to be the bearer of his country's message.

A backward glance suggests, furthermore, that in the past century most major figures of literature have functioned outside—and often in opposition to—the main tendencies of their society. This holds as true for Emerson, Thoreau, Whitman, Hawthorne, and Melville as for the Bohemians of the 1920's. "A piece of peculiarly bad advice is constantly given to modern writers. . . ." G. K. Chesterton has written somewhere "—that they should adapt themselves to the *spirit of the age.* If there is one thing that has made shipwreck of mankind from the beginning it has been the spirit of the age, which always means exaggerating still further something that is grossly exaggerated already."

Doubtless the Cold War poses special problems for an artist in a free society, and John Reed's conversion to communism does not recommend itself as a model. But isn't it possible that the Great Reconciliation has gone too far, and that in victory Bohemia has suffered its greatest defeat? If the tastes of Jacqueline Bouvier Kennedy are a felicitous sign of Bohemia's new respectability, there are other less creditable symptoms. It ought to be a subject for rueful meditation that the best known egghead of the 1950's was a young Villager who was a little too heartfelt about participating in the American Dream. The name was Charles Van Doren.

13 /

Who Killed the Bull Moose?

New truth always begins in a minority of one.
—HAROLD J. LASKI

AMONG ITS OTHER DISTINCTIONS, the year 1960 marked the final collapse of the American third-party tradition. On April 19, the last member of the Socialist Party to hold important elective office voluntarily retired. The departure of Mayor Frank P. Zeidler of Milwaukee was duly reported in *The New York Times*, a small item between the obituary and shipping pages. Not long afterward, the party of Eugene Debs and Norman Thomas decided, for the first time in six decades, not to participate in the Presidential election. Television reporters used the announcement as a "kicker" to round out the newscast, something on a par with Grandma Moses' hundredth birthday or the sixth marriage of a movie idol.

If it were needed, a note of finality was provided by Congress in its special rump session in August. The "equal time" provision of the Federal Communication Act was suspended for the campaign, meaning that broadcasters would not have to provide free time to the remaining

splinter sects—the Prohibitionists, Vegetarians, Trotsky-
ites, and the pertinacious Socialist Labor Party. If any
candidate was to receive free time on Channel Seven, his
brand name would have to be standardized.

This only confirmed what the country had come to take
for granted. In the past three Presidential elections minor
parties have served chiefly as an irritant for the huge computer machines on election night. While few were looking,
America became the only Western democracy without
any meaningful minor parties. Tiny Holland, which could
be tucked into a Texas county, has had as many as forty
political parties, but in the sprawling United States there
now is seemingly room for only two. And the paradox is
that the minor parties had dropped out of sight at the
very time when the Republicans and Democrats had become more alike than ever before.

I I

What happened to the third parties? Surely their disappearance warrants more attention. In the nineteenth
century, minor parties rose and fell with the regularity of
cloudbursts on a prairie. There were local parties like the
Anti-Monopolists, the Equal Rights Party, the Working-
men's Party, the Honest Men's Party of Massachusetts,
and the Readjusters of Virginia. Nationally, a virtually
unbroken sequence of third parties left their mark on
politics: the Anti-Masons, the Know-Nothings, the Liberty
Party, the Free-Soil Party, the Liberal Republicans, the
Greenbackers, and the Populists. They continued to flourish in this century. In 1912, the Socialists could claim
1,039 office holders in state legislatures and city councils,
while thirteen dailies and some 300 weeklies publicized

the party gospel. That year, Eugene Debs drew nearly a million votes, and Theodore Roosevelt polled four million votes as a Bull Moose candidate for the Presidency. During the 1930's, state third parties added to the ferment of the time: the Wisconsin Progressives, the Minnesota Farmer-Laborites, the New York American Labor Party. The final thundershower came in 1948, when the Wallace Progressives and the Dixiecrats each received a million votes. After that the tradition drizzled out until the Socialists reached a pathetic low of 2,044 votes in 1956.

One obvious reason for the demise of the minor parties is prosperity. Another is the adoption of the reforms first advocated by the dissidents. Again and again, third parties have advanced and developed a demand for a new proposal, only to see the Democrats and Republicans claim credit for its adoption. One has only to glance at the Populist platform of 1892 or the Socialist program of 1928 to see how many ideas given currency by third parties were adopted—"stolen," in the view of the dissidents—by other politicians. Norman Thomas tells the story of a Democratic candidate for the Assembly in a Brooklyn district who informed an outdoor rally: "Now, folks, you remember I used to tell you this here old age assistance was socialistic. It ain't anymore. The Democratic Party has endorsed it."

And no doubt the small parties themselves were unable to adjust themselves to the structure of American politics. The openness of our political system, the lack of ideological compartments, the fluid factionalism within each major party—these obstacles were too great for the insurgents. As Daniel Bell points out, the Socialists were unable to decide whether to play pragmatic politics or whether to remain pure and sectarian. In the politics of opportunism, the third parties were undercut at every turn by the shrewd managers who knew more about precincts than dialectics.

But when all this is said, the mystery remains. We have been prosperous before, the institutional barriers have existed for some time, and by no means all of the third-party proposals have been adopted. In Canada, a country like our own in so many respects, two significant minor parties—the socialistic CCF and the Social Credit Party—are active in provincial politics and make their voices heard in Ottawa.

Viewed from a different angle, isn't it possible that the answer lies in our becoming a mass society? Essentially, the third parties were as much cultural as political phenomena—they were the offshoots of a looser, more multifarious society in which two major parties, no matter how many factions each might contain, could not serve as the sole vehicles of political action. In a mass society, the supermarket crowds out the marginal items in politics as well as canned goods, and it is a nuisance to give "equal time" to eccentric little groups.

III

The third parties, in this view, were the expression of a plural society in which regionalism, ethnic factors, and differing class psychologies played a greater part in politics. To take an obvious example, the Populists, Dixiecrats, and Middle Western Progressives were all movements with a definable regional flavor. The stereotype of the typical Populist was of a hayseed who blamed Wall

Street and the Eastern "goldbugs" for all his woes. But the farmers—those who are left, at any rate—are no longer isolated from urban culture; they look at the same TV horse-operas as their city cousins.

Less widely known is the extent to which the melting pot contributed to third parties. Consider the Socialists. The movement was launched by German émigrés in the 1850's, and the party never wholly lost its "foreign" flavor. During its bumper years, the membership was an amalgam of native-born dissenters, many of whom had roots in the Populist movement, and of the foreign-born who had brought a socialist tradition to the New World. As Wilbur E. Moore points out in a sociological analysis of the party,

> The affiliated foreign-language groups provided one of the most dependable and numerically stable elements in the American Socialist Party. Their Socialist allegiance was clearly in terms of Old World ideas and conditions, given superficial validity in the American scene by the exploitation practiced on immigrants of all political persuasions or none.

It is suggestive that the only two Socialists elected to Congress were Victor Berger of Milwaukee and Meyer London of New York, the one a representative of a Germanic community and the other a spokesman for the Jewish immigrants on the East Side. Perhaps this immigrant coloration helps to explain why the American Socialists, unlike their comrades in France, Great Britain, and Germany, voted as a party to oppose World War I. More than their European brethren, the American Socialists could subscribe to the thesis that the workingman knows no country. As a result of this anti-war position, the party lost much of its native-born following. By 1919, the Socialists were a veritable Tower of Babel; 57,000 members (or 53 per cent of the total) belonged to foreign-language federations—Russian, Ukrainian, South Slavik, Finnish, Lithuanian, and Lettish.

Scarcely a radical movement in the past half century has not been indebted to the melting pot. The agrarian insurgents in Minnesota, Wisconsin, and North Dakota drew much of their support from Scandinavian and German ethnic groups. Even the Wobblies, so often described as an indigenous movement, were in part an ethnic phenomenon. No doubt the Industrial Workers of the World did have a native-born following, particularly in the mines and lumber camps of the West. But the testimony of Ralph Chaplin, the Wobbly leader and author of the song "Solidarity Forever," must be given weight. In his autobiography, Chaplin recalls:

Although Chicago [in 1914] was the general headquarters of the IWW, there was no English-speaking branch in town. The Jewish recruiting union had its hall on Twelfth Street, not far from where I worked. About a block beyond was the Russian IWW Propaganda Branch. . . . Both halls were lined with books, revolutionary papers, magazines printed in every language but English. The Jewish Wobblies sang Joe Hill's hobo songs, but the *Tovarischi* disdained them. They had songs of their own.

IV

The class psychology, too, was different. While America never possessed a proletariat in the European sense, there was a submerged working class in both town and rural area. The CIO had not been born, and the AFL was largely indifferent to the plight of those in the lower depths. Here was the electorate of the dispossessed that gave radicalism its cause and following.

Few realize that the pinkest state in the Union was once Oklahoma. An amiable German immigrant named Oscar Ameringer was to an important degree responsible. In his autobiography, *If You Don't Weaken*, Ameringer recalls his introduction to Oklahoma when he arrived as a Socialist organizer in 1907:

> I saw humanity at its lowest possible level of degradation and decay. I saw smug, well-dressed, overly well-fed hypocrites march to church on sabbath day, Bibles under their arm, praying for God's kingdom on earth while fattening like latter-day cannibals on the share croppers. I saw . . . as wretched a set of abject slaves as ever walked the face of the earth, anywhere, or at any time. . . . Up to then, I had been a part-time world-saver. Now I was a professional, on full time, and in every fiber of my being.

Notwithstanding his seraphic face, Ameringer proved to be an effective agent for socialism. At high tide, the Socialist vote in Oklahoma was nearly a third of the total cast. And this in a state where, as Ameringer put it, the people "were not wops or bohunks. They were not Jewish needle slaves. . . . They were more American than the population of any present-day New England town."

Encounters like these created a sense of The Enemy among Socialists, a sense vividly expressed in the titles of contemporary muckraking novels—*The Octopus, The Iron Heel, The Jungle*. The mood of the period is conveyed by the second stanza of Chaplin's "Solidarity Forever":

Is there aught we hold in common with the greedy parasite
Who would lash us into serfdom and would crush us
    with his might?
Is there anything left for us but to organize and fight?

In the fullness of time, The Enemy has changed from an octopus to a mother hen. Most Americans, Dr. Gallup informs us, regard themselves as members of the middle class, and the dispossessed have shown new tendencies unforeseen by Ameringer or Chaplin. Rather than class war, the specter of class collaboration is haunting the country—the specter of powerful unions and powerful corporations ganging up on the consumer. What has emerged today, Peter Drucker contends, is a way of life "beyond capitalism and socialism. It is a new society transcending both." And within the framework of this new society, the status scramble has replaced the class struggle which once gave an impetus to third party politics.

V

Somewhat the same problem is posed by this trend to monopoly in business and politics. Where do new ideas come from? Who is going to take up the innovatory role of the minor parties—and of the smaller businesses? The auto industry provides a case in point. When the compact car was pioneered by Nash Rambler, the titans of Detroit were scornful of the idea. Their polls showed, we were informed, that the American people really wanted those chrome-bedecked block-long behemoths. Indeed, the giant firms were so bemused by polls that the Ford Motor Company created a new line of cars in which every detail, from dashboard to tailpipe, was based on depth interviews. Thus,

Nash produced the Rambler; Ford gave us the Edsel.

The analogy with politics is evident. Big political parties, like big business, move slowly and take a chance only when the polls augur favorably. Mavericks, like American Motors, are needed to prod the giants and to draw attention to unmet demands. In economics we have an antitrust program aimed at discouraging monopoly and preserving smaller competitors. But we have no such program in politics, and we have no successor to the extinct third parties. We have only General Motors and Ford. The Fund for the Republic could do worse with its money than to underwrite a new party headed by someone who is irreverent about polls—someone, say, like George Romney, President of American Motors (Nash). Indeed, Mr. Romney, who has been active in Michigan politics as a kind of "third force," shows the proper spirit. "America's rendezvous with destiny is threatened, but not lost," Mr. Romney said at Mackinac in 1959. "It is threatened by a lack of basic political choice—lack of sufficient concern to cause us to risk and sacrifice for principles that have proven indispensable in man's pursuit of life, liberty, and happiness."

14 /

Signposts to Futopia

> The trouble with our age is all signposts and no
> destination.
>
> —LOUIS KRONENBERGER

Bᴜᴛ ᴛʜᴇ ᴍᴏsᴛ sᴏᴍʙᴇʀ and suggestive change in our society involves nothing so worldly as the passing of third-party politicians. Instead, it has been the destruction of a country that never existed. The country is Utopia, which served for so long as the symbol of Western man's faith in his future. Its disappearance is portentous enough, but an even more ominous phenomenon has been its replacement with a new kind of imagined society which, instead of depicting the possibilities of earthly bliss, serves only as a lens through which every barbarity of our age is magnified. This concept of a malignant future is so alien to our thinking that we do not have a word to describe what Max Eastman has called the "inverse Utopia." Perhaps "Futopia" would be appropriate.

The boundaries of Futopia are clearly marked in six novels published during the 1950's. While most of the Futopias abound in technical marvels, the fruits of science

only underscore the irony of the self-defeat of man's aspirations. All the Futopias share three themes: the degra-
dation of the individual, the perversion of reason and
science, and the absence of hope. The Heavenly City of
generations past had become an inferno of futility.

I I

This despairing vision is exemplified by one of the most
widely read of the new Futopias, David Karp's *One*. The
theme is the annihilation of the individuality of an obscure
professor who is guilty of holding heretical notions of self-
importance. He is haled before the Department of Internal
Examination, and his old identity, in the words of his in-
quisitor, is "pulverized." He is clothed with a completely
new personality in order to eliminate the heresy. However,
even in his new life as a clerk, signs of vanity still peep
through. In the end, he is destroyed as a menace to the
state.

In *One*, violence and barbarity are hidden beneath a
façade of benevolent paternalism; in another Futopia, the
barbarism is thrust into open view. Ray Bradbury's *Fahrenheit 451* pictures a Futopia where firemen no longer ex-
tinguish flames but start them—to burn books (451 degrees
is the temperature at which paper burns). Ownership of
any book is forbidden, on the plausible theory that books
stimulate dissatisfaction and critical thinking. As a sub-
stitute, wall-sized TV, ear-plug radios, and narcotizing
soap operas are provided. The hero, a fireman, rebels, is
caught owning books, and escapes shortly before an atomic
raid levels his country.

Atomic warfare is also an ingredient of the most grisly
of the Futopias, Bernard Wolfe's *Limbo*. In the world of

1990, shortly after the Third World War, a citizen's social status is determined by his number of missing limbs. Voluntary amputation is encouraged by such slogans as "He Who Has Arms Is Armed," "Make Disarmament Last," "Arms or the Man." The goal is to stifle aggressive impulses; the chief debate is whether artificial limbs circumvent the "disarmament" code. One extremist faction practices total amputation (including castration) in order to achieve "total immobilization." This Futopia's streets are lined with "quadra-amps," nesting in baskets, who proselyte pedestrians in high-pitched voices. Yet amputation proves futile; the story closes amid another global war.

Less repulsive, though scarcely more optimistic, is Kurt Vonnegut's *Player Piano*. This Futopia relies more on vacuum tubes than on surgery, and is devoted to the principle that the "average" man is obsolete. Society is stratified on the basis of intelligence quotient (each citizen's I.Q. is filed for public inspection). IBM machines dictate which persons shall go to college and become engineers—the elite. Since machinery has displaced manual labor, the bulk of the population broods in idleness and frustration—sometimes doing "made work" to leaven boredom. Rebellion finally breaks out, but it is promptly quelled by the machines who are like men and the men who are like machines.

In Gore Vidal's *Messiah*, a new cult springs up in California based on the premise that "it is good to die." The Messiah of the movement is John Cave, a brooding employee of Whittaker and Dormer, Funeral Directors, who mesmerizes the country with his sermons on the pleasures of death. Soon, suicide centers are thriving, Christmas becomes Cavesday, and Cavesword sweeps a world yearning for Death.

But the most dismal of the new Futopias is *The Space*

Merchants, by Frederik Pohl and C. M. Kornbluth. Here we are confronted with a world ruled by advertising agencies in which the Consumer (the lowest rank in the hierarchy) is assailed by commercials wherever he looks or whatever he does. The one hopeful note in this appalling Futopia is that the underground opposition, the "Consies" (*i.e.,* conservationists) manage to escape on a space ship bound for Venus.

III

So runs the beguiling picture of the future evolved by American novelists in the past decade. It would be superficial and inaccurate to dismiss these books as topical polemics aimed at Communism or McCarthyism. The vision of Futopia is not bounded by simple political stereotypes, but instead embraces the larger problems of living with industrialism, with its standardization, its blend of social science and mass culture, with its manipulation. Ultimately, the roots of Futopia reach back to the eighteenth and nineteenth centuries.

Although philosophers since Plato have devised plans for an ideal society, Utopia in the modern sense was derived from the machine and from the belief in progress. The premise was that human reason could be used to redesign a society without poverty or crime—a Heavenly City on this earth. So attractive was this idea that during the 1830's and 1840's more than a hundred secular Utopias were founded in America by the followers of Robert Owen, Albert Brisbane, and Margaret Fuller. "We are a little worried here with numberless projects of social reform," Emerson wrote Carlyle in 1840. "Not a reading man but has a draft of a new community in his waistcoat pocket."

With few exceptions, the Utopian communities dissolved as quickly as they were formed. But the impulse remained alive. When Edward Bellamy, in 1887, wrote *Looking Backward*, the very archetype of nineteenth-century Utopianism, enthusiasm for his vision exceeded his fondest hopes. Half a million copies of the book sold within a year; Nationalist Clubs, dedicated to hurrying in the Golden Age by nationalizing business, sprang up everywhere. Between 1888 and 1900, no fewer than forty Utopian novels —most of them directly inspired by Bellamy—came from the presses. Utopia had come a considerable distance since Sir Thomas More coined the term in 1516; to countless dreamers, the ideal society was close at hand.

Indeed, Theodor Hertzka, an Austrian economist who wrote *Freeland* in 1890, was planning a colonizing venture to put his theories into practice. Eugene Debs and other Socialists were considering the same plan in America in 1897. As the nineteenth century closed, millions shared the hopes of Bellamy, who silenced sceptics by saying, "Our children will live to see it."

In many respects, H. G. Wells personified this Utopian tradition. Humanist, scientist, and socialist, Wells wrote the classic *A Modern Utopia* in 1905 and continued the tradition in the appropriately titled *The World Set Free* (1914) and *Men Like Gods* (1923). But some time after the "war to end wars" (it was Wells, significantly, who originated the phrase), the vision palled; and Wells, the lifelong Utopian, despaired of man. In his last book, *Mind at the End of Its Tether* (1946), he concluded bitterly: "The end of everything we call life is close at hand and cannot be evaded." What had happened to Utopia? What events mark the immeasurable distance between Bellamy in 1887 and Wells in 1946?

In a sense, the event that destroyed Utopia was its very realization. The fundamental prescription of traditional Utopias was planning—total planning. Through planning, argued Bellamy, an economy of abundance would replace the squalor of the laissez-faire world of 1887, and enable each individual to achieve his potential. The argument was plausible in the planless wastes of nineteenth-century capitalism. Since large-scale planning had never been attempted in an industrial society, there was no experience to draw upon; Bellamy's Utopia was like an exercise in social metaphysics.

Bellamy never lived to see the Russian Revolution—but H. G. Wells did. In his *Experiment in Autobiography* (1934), he recorded his reactions shortly after his second trip to the Soviet Union:

> . . . I felt that Russia had let me down, whereas I suppose the truth of what has happened is that I had allowed my sanguine and impatient temperament to anticipate understandings and lucidities that cannot arrive for many years. . . . I had started out to find a short cut [to Utopia] and discovered that . . . there is no short cut. . . .

Thus the formula of traditional Utopianism, upon its realization, raised new questions and left old ones unsettled. As the implications of planning in an industrial society became clearer, it was a Soviet citizen, appropriately, who wrote the first Futopian novel.

I V

The story of Eugene Zamiatin bears a strong resemblance to that of Boris Pasternak. Like Pasternak, Zamiatin was a writer who sympathized with the Revolution yet could not become a total convert. In 1920, Zamiatin considered the threat to individuality implicit in Soviet planning and set his musings down in a short novel entitled We. Its satire was too sharp for Russian consumption, but overseas publication was possible and an English translation appeared in 1924. Like Pasternak, Zamiatin's reputation is based on the translation of a work that has yet to appear in the author's own country.

In his extraordinary novel, Zamiatin anticipated almost every fear that subsequent Futopians were to dwell upon. The hero of We, a nameless Number (as citizens of this Futopia are known) called D-503, lives in the perfectly planned state. The daily routine of every Number is regulated by a Table of Hours; all Numbers arise, eat, work, and play by the same schedule—and are allowed one scant hour a day in which they can pull the blinds in their homes of glass. Yet the benevolent Guardian class is not without worries; occasionally "fancy" seizes the mind of a wayward Number. Therefore the Guardians perfect an operation for removing "fancy" altogether; the event is announced in a passage worthy of quotation:

REJOICE!

For from now on we are *perfect!* Before today your own creation, engines, were more perfect than you.

WHY?

For every spark from a dynamo—is a spark of pure reason; each motion of a piston—a pure syllogism. . . . The beauty of a mechanism lies in its immutable, precise rhythm, like that of a pendulum. But have you not become as precise as a pendulum, you who are brought up on the system of Taylor?
Yes, but there is a difference.

MECHANISMS HAVE NO FANCY

Did you ever notice a pump cylinder during its work show upon its face a wide, distant, sensuously-dreaming smile? . . .

NO!

Yet on your faces (you may well blush with shame!) the Guardians have seen more and more frequently those smiles and they have heard your sighs. . . .

It is not your fault; you are ill. And the name of your illness is

FANCY

. . . It is the last barricade on our road to happiness. *Rejoice! This Barricade Has Been Blasted at Last! The Road Is Open!* The latest discovery of our State science is that there is a center for fancy—a miserable little nervous knot in the lower region of the frontal lobe of the brain. A triple treatment of this knot with X-rays will cure you of fancy—

FOREVER!

You are perfect; you are mechanized; the road to hun- dred per cent happiness is open! Hasten then all of you, young and old, hasten to undergo the Great Operation! . . . Long live the Well-Doer!

Before the brains of all Numbers are irradicably washed, an abortive revolt breaks out. The book closes with the march of Numbers to the Great Operation as the rebel leader is publicly liquidated. (The fate of Zamiatin pro- vides a poignant footnote. In 1929 he was accused of "un- belief and nonacceptance of the social revolution," with the case largely resting on *We*. In 1931, he became an exile; he died in Paris in 1937.)

V

To a great extent, subsequent Futopias are only an elaboration of *We*. The regimentation of individuals, the rule of a mysterious elite, the tyranny of science, the closing of all escapes—all these themes are the staples of later Futopias. In terms of emphasis, however, there is an important exception: If one aspect of Futopia was disclosed in Soviet planning, a second was realized in the technological abundance of America. Traditional Utopians such as Bellamy and Wells founded their hopes on the potential blessings of science. Yet, as H. G. Wells confessed in 1942:

> These new powers, inventions, contrivances and methods, are not the unqualified enrichment of normal life that we had expected. They are hurting, injuring and frustrating us increasingly. . . . We are only beginning to realize that the cornucopia of innovation may perhaps prove far more dangerous than benevolent.

Aldous Huxley led the way in making Futopian mockery of the unexpected fruits of science. In *Brave New World* (1932), the target is not Russia so much as America; the villain is not Marx but Henry Ford. If *Looking Backward* prophesied the radio, *Brave New World* adumbrates the "feely," a form of movies now only a dimension away. The novel is a caricature of an affluent society in which the prosperity made possible by technology serves to corrupt and imprison instead of liberate. As one character explains, "You can't have a lasting civilization without plenty of pleasant vices." The only victim is humanity, represented by Savage, who hangs himself to escape Huxley's pneumatic wonderland.

With the rise of Hitler, the third strand of Futopianism appears: the revelation that it was possible for an advanced Western country to revert to barbarism, and that the traditional democracies initially seemed too selfish or shortsighted to unite against an atavistic neighbor. This theme was given Futopian form, fittingly, by a Czech, Karel Capek, whose *War with the Newts* (1937) is a forgotten minor classic of the genre. Capek, of course, originated the word "robot" in his play, *R.U.R.* (1921), and prophesied the rivalry of the great powers over atomic weapons in his novel, *Krakatit* (1924). In his *War with the Newts*, Capek describes the discovery on a Pacific island of a breed of salamanders that were as large as men, seemingly harmless and easy to train. The newts work with machine-like efficiency, and soon various schemes for commercial exploitation of this cheap labor were devised. As the newts multiply and prepare for revolt, they are strengthened by their victims—the Western democracies—because the pursuit of national advantage makes common action impossible. Capek died on December 25, 1938, after the Munich Pact. A biographer notes: "He died of no specific ailment. Grief killed him: there was no one left to warn."

With the advent of the Second World War, the Futopian gloom deepened. Huxley predicted, "The horror may be upon us within a single century." And George Orwell moved the date to 1984 and reached the ultimate in perverting original Utopianism with his savage portrait of a society like "a boot stamping on the human face—forever."

By 1955, the Futopian bookshelf was sufficiently large for a British author, R. C. Churchill, to write a 192-page *Short History of the Future*, complete with maps and mock-scholarly footnotes. Although there is an occasional cheerful note, the immediate future of the West as seen by Mr. Churchill is a synthesis of the Futopias of Orwell, Huxley, Bradbury, Karp, Vonnegut, and others. Scarcely more comforting was Sir Charles Darwin's *The Next Million Years* (1952) which sees the disagreeable present as a Golden Age and little else but decline ahead. In the 1950's Futopia had become as real and imminent as the earthly paradise envisaged by Bellamy and Wells a half century before.

V I

The diminishing distance between science fiction and fact can be seen in the case of the "people machine." In "All the Troubles of the World," a short story written by Isaac Asimov in 1958, we meet Multivac—"the giant computer that had grown in fifty years until its ramifications had filled Washington, D.C., to the suburbs and had reached out tendrils into every city and town on Earth." Each day, an army of civil servants feeds new data into Multivac in order to help it correlate four billion sets of facts about individual human beings and by extrapolation thus predict the events of the day. Cases of crime were anticipated by Multivac, economic decisions made, and even answers to individual problems provided by substations located in each city.

The same year that Mr. Asimov's story appeared in *Super-Science Fiction*, Dr. William McPhee, a director of Columbia University's Bureau of Applied Social Research, began working on a theory needed to build a computer model of the U.S. television public. After consultation, however, Dr. McPhee decided to abandon the TV project and instead build a model of the American electorate, a program which interested Democrats had agreed to finance.

According to Thomas B. Morgan, in an article in *Harper's* (January, 1961), a memo was sent in 1959 to Thomas K. Finletter, a member of the Democratic Advisory Council, which said: "It is possible to develop a computer program which will predict the result of alternative campaign strategies from limited public-opinion-poll data and do so in a matter of minutes with greater detail about different states and groups of voters."

Thus was born the "people machine," which has been described by Dr. Harold Lasswell of Yale as the "A-bomb of the social sciences." As carried out by the Simulmatics Corporation in 1960, the project involved feeding the results of sixty-six nation-wide opinion surveys carried out since 1952 into an IBM 704 computer. To simulate the electorate, 480 groups—"voter types"—were programmed for the computer, *e.g.*: Eastern, rural, well-off, Protestant, male; Midwestern, small-town, poor, Catholic, female; Western, metropolitan, Jewish, male, etc. Then, the machine was asked to forecast the possible consequences of different campaign strategies.

It is not known to what extent the Kennedy campaign used data from the "people machine." However, it seems clear that Robert Kennedy, the President's campaign manager, did receive reports based on the computer's projections concerning foreign affairs, the TV debates, the religious issue, and campaign techniques. Whatever Robert Kennedy did with the data, there was a parallel between the IBM recommendations, as reported in *Harper's*, and actual election tactics. Here is an example of a report provided by the Simulmatics Corporation:

Nixon has been less effective on TV than Kennedy. The crucial TV debates are therefore a risk for him. Should he be able to trap Kennedy into approaching the debates at his own level of super-coolness, he can "win" the debates. The danger to Nixon is that Kennedy can make use of his more personable traits—including a range of emotions such as fervor, humor, friendship, and spirituality beyond the expected seriousness and anger—and thus cause Nixon to "lose" the debates.

This simulation of voter response is said to be the first of its kind, and the implications reach far beyond "image" research during a campaign. As Thomas B. Morgan points out, "It will speed up the process of discovering a consensus concerning the goals of our society. It will compel leaders to refine their decisions because they will at last have accurate information about public opinion." President Eisenhower sought to define national goals by appointing a committee; will President Kennedy ask a machine? Surely this would be the ultimate triumph of supermarket politics.

The theoretical potential of predictor machines is virtually unlimited—and in theory the machines could compose sonnets and symphonies as well as guide events. Denis Gabor, Professor of Applied Electron Physics at the University of London, writing in *Encounter* (May, 1960), states that of all electronic inventions now within viewing distance, the predictors will have the greatest influence on civilization. The universal simulator—Mr. Asimov's Multivac—is wholly possible. Indeed, the machine can take into account human reactions to its prophecies, and if the computer's reputation is good, its predictions could be blindly followed. Professor Gabor remarks: "The machine, being a learning machine, will soon notice that everything it says goes, and from that moment on there is no guarantee against its going astray. Absolute power will corrupt not only men but machines!" (In Mr. Asimov's story,

Multivac is finally asked what *it* wants; after some click-ing, a card popped out, reading: "I want to die.")

Professor Gabor's thoughtful article, after noting that in thirty years no optimistic Utopias have been written, goes on to ask:

> Who is responsible for this tragi-comedy of Man frus-trated by success? If the intellectuals at the other side of the fence say that the fault is ours, of the scientists and inventors, we are not in a position to deny it. But instead of bowing our heads in shame, I think we ought to return the accusation and ask: "Who has left Mankind without a Vision?" . . .
>
> Some thirty years ago the French critic Julien Benda wrote a famous book, *La Trahison des Clercs,* in which he accused the *"clercs,"* the writers and thinkers . . . of "treason" by embracing dogma of one sort or another, or the creed of extreme nationalism. Today we are faced with a new treason of the *clercs*—oh, nothing as crude and criminal as the treason of the French intellectuals Barrès and Maurras—no treason by commission, but only by omission: by not giving us a vision for which to live.

15 /

The Two Worlds

Sometimes I thank God for the Russians—their rapid
progress may even make economic growth, risk, and
adventure essential, if not respectable, here.

—ADLAI STEVENSON

"How FASHIONS CHANGE! Ten years ago left-
wing convictions were modish among 'well-informed public
opinion'. . . . Now the right thing is, not to be a Conservative (that would be too positive an attitude) but to show
a studied indifference to party politics, and to express
quizzical doubts about the socialist belief that human society can be improved by political action."

So R. H. S. Crossman wrote in 1955—a Briton speaking
about the British. But variations on the same theme can
be found in hundreds of articles in American magazines
during the past decade. Not the least of the ties that now
bind us to Britain is the common language of disillusion.
For in Britain, too, campaign strategy in politics has passed
from the political believers to the mass market analyst.

In an article in *The Reporter*, George Steiner has offered
a persuasive analysis of the decline of the Labour Party.

As with their American counterparts, the party's old guard
has been unable to cope with the comparative affluence of
the electorate. "The language of Bevan and Morrison is
no longer meaningful to the young," Mr. Steiner contends,
"it speaks to the harsh remembrance of the old." The
Tories, however, have become the champions of the consumer society and have "identified themselves with the
jovial vulgarity and materialism that characterize the new
England. . . . Indeed, if one had to choose the emblem of
the Conservative victory [in 1959], it could well be the TV
screen." In that campaign, we are informed by Mr. Steiner,
"the most refined techniques of market research were used
to discover what image of the party and its program would
have the strongest consumer appeal." Before long, no doubt,
British and American politicians will begin swapping opinion polls—the ultimate expression of Anglo-American unity.

Britain, for that matter, is only a step ahead of Western
Europe. In West Germany, the Social Democrats have
come closest to imitating the American model. While the
British Socialists are badly split among themselves on what
to do with the legacy of radicalism, their German comrades
have pretty much scrapped the entire ideology of socialism.
There are special reasons for this: the success of free enterprise in West Germany, the nightmarish proximity of the
East German People's Republic, and the tragic burden of
the past. For the Social Democrats, the process of change
culminated in November, 1960, when the party discarded
the remnants of its Marxist heritage and rallied behind
Mayor Willy Brandt, the estimable champion of Berlin.
R. H. S. Crossman, who was present at the party conference in Hanover, described the climactic moment: "Finally
. . . the curtain was drawn aside, and there before us was
the new image of a new party, designed on the pattern of

the American Democrats and headed by a new leader, unmistakably modelling himself on Mr. Kennedy."

When Mr. Crossman, a Labour member of Parliament, remarked to one of the Social Democratic leaders that there was little in the platform that Chancellor Adenauer's Christian Democratic Union could not endorse, he received this reply:

> Our aim is to bring ourselves as close alongside our opponents of the CDU as we possibly can. That is why we have become not only a party of free enterprise, without any commitment to further public ownership, but have abandoned all our attacks on Adenauer's foreign policy and are now insisting on bipartisanship in foreign affairs. Later on in the campaign, however, we may well distance ourselves a little from our opponents if it is tactically desirable.

Karl Kautsky or Rosa Luxemburg might be appalled, but this outlook would be wholly familiar to an American politician. It is the strategy known as pre-empting the center, a tactic for which, in view of Germany's past, there may be a good deal to say. The leader of the opposition in West Germany could choose worse models to emulate than John F. Kennedy.

II

But viewed in a larger context, this tendency in the West is in paradoxical contrast to developments elsewhere in the world. In the overdeveloped countries, the shrewd politician seeks to pre-empt the center; in underdeveloped regions, the leader frequently must sound like an extremist even if he is not one. Nothing could be more fatal for a politician in Venezuela, Ghana, or Iraq than to be called a safe and solid moderate. For Utopia, in the sense that this concept embodies belief in a planned society roughly along socialist lines, may have dropped out of NATO— but it is still a vivid symbol in the underdeveloped world.

A recent dispatch from Jakarta in *The New York Times*, headlined "Sukarno Offers Socialist Utopia," bears on the point:

> An Indonesian Utopia, complete with husband and modern kitchen for every woman, is being advertised by President Sukarno in a campaign to rally support for Indonesian socialism. Life under socialism, the President assures the women, will have it all over capitalism. . . . Under socialism there will be so many modern conveniences— electricity, radios, the latest kitchen appliances—that wives will have lots of free time for "companionship, motherhood and love," the President says.

The worldly may snicker at this AC-DC paradise, but the snicker would be the measure of the political and emotional distance between the rich and poor countries. I have not been to Africa, Asia, or the Middle East, but I have had some firsthand contact with Latin America. A journey to Latin America is like falling through a trapdoor into the past. You are confronted with the kind of squalor that Oscar Ameringer found in Oklahoma generations ago. The major cities of the region fester with slums, and beneath the neon signs advertising North American luxuries you may find an uprooted peasant whose expression plainly says "Yankee, go home."

While the language of Marxism sounds archaic in the United States, it has quite a different ring in Latin America. There, words like *imperialism, proletariat, oligarchy, peasant,* and *exploitation* seem to mirror reality, and the phrase *class struggle* lacks satiric overtones. It is not surprising that

Marxist jargon is so endemic among students and intellectuals.

But there is a double irony at the root of Latin American radicalism. First, the ferment in the region seems to owe far more to Madison Avenue than to the Kremlin. No Communist spy could stir up more discontent with the status quo than the advertisements in *Life* or the alluring window of one of the many Sears, Roebuck stores in Latin America. Yet, though we excel in quickening appetites, we fail dismally in showing how to satisfy the very demands our hucksters have stimulated. Thus we open the way for the Communists who speak in accents of change and who offer a blueprint for Utopia—a Utopia stocked with the wares of *our* supermarket.

A second irony is that we have been most successful in spreading the most subversive of technical knowledge—the health and sanitary measures which raise birth rates and prolong life. Perhaps because medicine is the safest and least controversial of philanthropic enterprises, our public health agencies have inundated Latin America with health projects. But there has been no comparable success in encouraging the technical skills which would make those whose lives have been saved glad to be alive. Latin America is the fastest-growing region in the world—but only in terms of population. The population in the area is now increasing at a rate five times greater than the rate of increase in goods and services. Thus, at the very time when expectations are the highest, the prospects are that Latin America's lot will worsen rather than improve.

This is the cauldron from which Fidel Castro emerged. Enough has been said of Castro's faults; doubtless he is irrational, demagogic, and dangerous. But what makes him especially dangerous is that while North Americans can't "understand" Castro's anger, many Latin Americans can. To this country, Castro has seemed like a stranger from another century, a zealot who is half-mad. What sane U.S. college student would attempt to overthrow a dictator with an "army" of only twelve men? Would any sophisticated intellectual believe that an old and corrupt society could be wholly transformed in a matter of a few years?

We are too wise to believe that, but while Castro is busy learning about the futility of political change, we stand a good chance of losing what remains of our influence in Latin America. The gulf between this country and its neighbors recalls Disraeli's definition of two nations "between whom there is no intercourse and no sympathy . . . as if they were dwellers in different zones, or inhabitants of different planets." As a character in one of Disraeli's novels exclaims: "The capitalist flourishes; we sink lower and lower . . . and yet they tell us that the interest of Capital and Labour are identical." It is as if Disraeli's description has been translated into international terms—with a vertical division between countries rather than a horizontal division within England. In Disraeli's time, the Chartists, also unreasonable fellows, were marching on London and demanding the franchise. In the two worlds, the latter-day Chartists are pounding at the gate and insisting that their voice be heard too. Over the years, the British were able to unite the two nations into one. Will we be able to do the same with the two worlds?

I I I

The obstacles are imposing. We are not psychologically attuned to dealing with revolutionaries, and we tend to think in short-run terms about limited objectives. In contrast, the Communists speak a language more beguiling to the impatient and impoverished. Moreover, the formulas of Marxism seem more plausible in underdeveloped countries than in the advanced industrial states which were supposed to lead the way to socialism. Finally, the Communist model of swift economic development seems more relevant to backward countries than the model offered by the West.

Still, the Communists have their problems and are scarcely ten feet tall. The dogmas of a theological state tend to blind the believer to disconcerting heresies, and encourage a rigidity of outlook and a manner of intolerance. There is also the reality of the Soviet state with its suffocating controls, and there is the colonial empire in Eastern Europe. And, as Russia too becomes a more affluent society, the revolutionary impetus slows down. We read with ill-concealed delight every report of bourgeois vices appearing in the Communist bloc. Supermarkets, jazz bands, beatniks, comic books, installment buying, and even ghost writers have cropped up in the Soviet orbit. In Poland, the Communist Party organ, *Trybuna Ludu,* recently described an all-out battle among the party elite over possession of the newest status symbol—a white telephone. Not long ago, this letter signed by three young teachers in Murmansk appeared in the official Soviet youth publication, *Komsomolskaya Pravda:*

> In the evenings, we often discuss the question: What is the meaning of life? Haven't we turned into Philistines? We appreciate, of course, that the main purpose confronting us is the building of communism, but each human being must have his own special purpose, of which he is really aware. We have no such purpose. What, therefore,

is the meaning of life? . . . We have no enthusiasm. In
fact, can enthusiasm exist these days?

Can the Smooth Commissar be far behind?

But it would be foolish to place too much hope in these
symptoms of agreeable degeneracy in the Soviet system.
After all, the Chinese Communists are still around. And
just as the presence of the Soviet Union makes this country
more energetic in doing what it should do anyway for the
less fortunate of the world, so the presence of the Chinese
will continue to add militance to the Russians.

If the obstacles are formidable to inspiring a missionary
zeal in the West, nonetheless the free world still commands
imposing resources. There is a reservoir of wealth and
skills which has been only partially tapped. And in the
United States there is an authentic revolutionary tradition
of anti-colonialism, land reform, egalitarianism, and welfare legislation which has potentially more to offer to the
underdeveloped countries than the spurious Soviet brand.

As evidence that free men can close the gap between the
two worlds in an efficient yet humane way, there is the
case of Puerto Rico, an island that one visitor described
a few years ago as the "Formosa of the New Deal." Under
the leadership of Governor Luis Muñoz-Marin, Puerto
Rico has diversified its economy, created an industrial base,
doubled its living standard, and achieved self-government
—and this has happened within two decades on an island
once known as "the stricken land," where the only resource
was an oversupply of labor. Governor Muñoz, a one-time
poet, Socialist, and Greenwich Villager, has made a success of Operation Bootstrap without resorting to the fire-
water of nationalism. Nor has there been any diminution
of the freedom of all citizens—from Catholic Bishops to

affluent millionaires—to denounce the government and all its works. Characteristically, the Governor has appointed Roger Baldwin, founder of the American Civil Liberties Union, as a watchdog for the dissenters.

This is the kind of revolution which the West must learn to export. It is a hopeful sign that one of Governor Muñoz-Marin's trusted lieutenants, Arturo Morales-Carrión, has come to Washington as Deputy Assistant Secretary of State for Inter-American Affairs. Not long after his arrival in the Capital, I spoke to Dr. Morales about his impressions of the Kennedy Administration. "Well, the mood in the Government is like that of Puerto Rico in 1940, when we were just beginning—but the mood of the public," he continued, "seems to trail behind." Surely the primary problem for Mr. Kennedy in the years ahead will be to persuade the country that the world cannot survive half in affluence and half in poverty, and that, as in Disraeli's time (but in Mr. Kennedy's words), "if a free society cannot help the many who are poor, it can never save the few who are rich."

AFTERWORD

The Sweet Smell of Excess

A certain element of excess seems to be a necessary
element in all greatness.

—ALFRED NORTH WHITEHEAD

H AD ANYTHING CHANGED? This was the question
that an observer might have found himself asking at the
Inaugural ceremonies in Washington on January 20, 1961.
The day was cold, bright, brittle. Around the Capitol, there
was a palpable sense that something new was beginning;
the clergymen seemed to offer inordinately long benedic-
tions, as if to make doubly sure that Providence was attentive. Then a hush came over the gathering when for a
moment it appeared that catastrophe might overtake Robert
Frost, whose presence had provided a grace note to the
occasion. But catastrophe was averted, and "The Gift Outright" came in measured tones. Above the rostrum sat the
potentates of Congress who gazed half-patronizingly at
the self-possessed young man who seemed more the spectator than the main event at his own Inaugural. Surely
Congress had not changed; if anything, the 1960 elections
had weeded out some of the mavericks who had lent life
to the preceding Congress. The tone of the incoming

Eighty-Seventh seemed as solid, safe, and sterilized as the new marble East Front of the Capitol on which the ceremony was taking place. It was not surprising when, a few days later, only a handful of votes saved the Kennedy program from likely extinction in the House Rules Committee.

As Mr. Kennedy rose to take the oath, the expression on President Eisenhower's face was a curious blend of the benign, the wistful, and paternal. Mr. Eisenhower had not changed, nor had the country's estimate of his capability. It was a truism that if the Constitution had not ruled out a third term, and if his party had prevailed on him to run, Mr. Eisenhower would have won hands down against any contender. The country, becalmed and contented, was still very much Eisenhower's America.

With the oath over, the Inaugural Address began, and it appeared that what *had* changed, more than anything else, was John F. Kennedy. He scarcely resembled the man who ran a teacup campaign in 1952 and then became known as the Senate's "gay young bachelor." Nor was it the man who had been faulted for his lack of valor during the McCarthy years. His voice now was insistent, like the thump of a drum, and there was a union of intelligence and authority in his manner. Only the incurably partisan could not have but wished him well.

The Address itself was as remarkable for what it left out as for what it contained. There was no reference to domestic affairs, but instead the speech was a commitment to a long, twilight struggle abroad—it was a declaration of interdependence, an announcement of union with a world from which America could no longer secede. The country had come a long way from the isolationist dream expressed in Washington's Farewell Address.

I I

How would the country take it? The circumstances of history seemed less kind to Mr. Kennedy than to Franklin Delano Roosevelt. When FDR took office in 1933, the crisis of the old order was plainly visible—closed banks, bread lines, Hoovervilles. There was a readiness for the changes that the times demanded. However, in 1961 the crisis was largely invisible; only the tip of the iceberg showed.

For eight years, the country's Administration had re-iterated the comforting message that America was the wisest and strongest land in the world. The voices of the opposition party in Congress, more often than not, were in muted agreement. An attitude of caution and timidity had become so ingrained in our politics that even the more daring figures seemed to acquiesce in the proposition that Red China did not exist, that military expedience justified alliances with tyrants, and that the key to containing Communism was mainly in more and bigger bombs.

It seemed as if something had gone awry with the American political equilibrium. Since checks and balances are interwoven in every branch of government, any change is difficult to bring about. If the system is to budge from dead center, it requires leaders who are willing to go beyond the existing consensus and take the risks of uttering unpalatable truths. Thus, though the structure of the system is moderate, any forward motion requires the lubricant of excess.

Yet in Congress in 1961, the words "excess" and "extremist" were regarded as noxious epithets, along with "doctrinaire." Among the liberals, the typical figure seemed to be a politician who made prudence the touchstone of his career, who—so it seemed—tried to embody the system of checks and balances within himself. The tone was set by the Vice President, who has made amply clear his disdain for the "ultra-liberals" and the "redhots." In the Official Inaugural Program, Lyndon B. Johnson expressed disgust with all questions of doctrine, saying, in an article entitled "My Political Philosophy": "I bridle at the very casualness with which we have come to ask each other, 'What is your political philosophy?' "

Assuredly, the system requires men of Mr. Johnson's temper. But what the Vice President has not seemed to appreciate is that the reason he can be a moderate is because there are others to his left and right. A compromiser can use his talents only when there is something to compromise. If it were not for a few committed voices to his left, Mr. Johnson himself might be considered a "redhot" too—a fate one would not lightly wish on the squire of Johnson City, Texas.

Our political equilibrium requires weights at the extremes to stay in balance. It needs the Wayne Morses and Barry Goldwaters as well as the mediators in the middle. In the coming years, those who take a position in advance of Mr. Kennedy's can serve as the indispensable scouts on the New Frontier. That the point should have to be made at all is a melancholy commentary on our present condition.

III

In seasons of change, there are anchors of permanence, and these include *The New York Times*. Still, there was an unexpected note on the front page of the *Times* this Inaugural day. "The problems before the Kennedy Administration on Inauguration Day are much more difficult than the Nation has yet come to believe," James Reston commented, "and in the long run the solutions are likely to be more radical than anything in American politics since the first administration of Franklin Delano Roosevelt."

Radical—the word had an odd sound in Washington, Anno Domini 1961. Yet one wondered if Mr. Reston, with his knack for detecting a trend, had not chosen the right word. As the nature of the problem confronting the West has come into clearer focus, the limitations of Dynamically Moderate Conservatism or Moderately Dynamic Liberalism have become more self-evident. With half the world yearning for a New Deal, it seemed unlikely that the cause of freedom would prevail by offering the ill-fed, the ill-housed, and the ill-treated preachments on moderation.

Mr. Reston did not define the term "radical," but the general meaning was clear enough. Four characteristics, though not exclusive to the American radical tradition, seem essential to it. First, the conviction that human intelligence can alter and improve the human environment; second, as the word itself implies, a willingness to go beyond fashionable slogans to underlying fundamentals; third, an experimental attitude to existing institutions; and finally, a sense of compassionate fraternity with the oppressed anywhere in the world.

On the first three counts, the Kennedy Administration has already shown promise of reawakening the dormant traditions of radicalism. As in few other administrations, the appointments have reflected a respect for intellectual ability and independence. ("It is a most radical experiment," Richard Rovere remarked in *The New Yorker*—the word seems to come easily again.) No less radical has been the freedom from cant in the President's utterances —and his respect for syntax. While the language of politics is filled with tactical ambiguities, Mr. Kennedy's prose can be as sharp as a scalpel when he chooses. And a spirit of innovation could be felt in Washington again, a city that had almost seemed to forget that the law of change is the law of life.

But it is on the final count that the prospects of the Kennedy Administration may well hinge. As the President took office, the country seemed to have reached the outer limits of privatism in virtually every aspect of life—in the arts and religion as well as in politics. "We talk about ourselves these days as if we were a completed society," Walter Lippmann wrote, "one which has achieved its purposes and has no further great business to transact." The country seemed less a nation than an aggregrate of private appetites, less a community than a cluster of private worlds swept along in a drift. The public was indifferent to politics, and the leadership seemed afraid to lead. It was as if Spengler was right, and the country was slowly sinking out of sight without even a decent final saturnalia. "In the most radical and revolutionary epoch of man's history, the dominant concerns of our leadership have been almost wholly defensive," Adlai Stevenson commented in *Foreign Affairs* in January, 1960.

Plainly, the great task before Mr. Kennedy is to reverse this tendency—a tendency of which the President himself is keenly aware. "It is one of the ironies of our time," he remarked in his State of the Union message

> that the techniques of a harsh and repressive system should be able to instill discipline and ardor into its servants—while the blessings of liberty have too often stood for privilege, materialism, and a life of ease.

But if he is to restore politics to the center of affairs, he will surely have to do more than to make the center the sole affair of politics. Circumstances—and the lethargy in Congress—may well dictate caution on some fronts, but if the same policy prevails on *all* fronts the path ahead could well become a middle-road leading nowhere. A bland and adroit managerialism, in sum, may not be enough to bestir the nation to the exertions worthy of a free people at their most perilous summit.

Acknowledgments and Sources

L IKE THE FEDERAL BUDGET, this book is burdened with debts, many of them difficult to repay. My first obligation is to the Washington *Post*, for generously permitting the leave of absence which enabled me to complete the book. My debt to my wife Sarah is only partly expressed in the dedication; she provided sane counsel and the ballast of a tranquil home.

A special word of thanks is due to Mrs. Beth Brod, who assisted on the research, contributed helpful ideas, and fathomed libraries for elusive data.

In addition, a host of friends and colleagues were kind enough to read parts of the book and offer valuable advice. I am especially indebted to Sidney Hyman, Amos Elon, Richard N. Goodwin, Victor Alba, and Susan Meyer. Errors of fact or judgment are of course the responsibility of a congenitally intemperate author.

Chapters three, five, and six appeared in somewhat different form as articles in *Commentary*, *Harper's*, and *The Progressive*. Parts of chapters one and fourteen appeared in *The Progressive* and *The Reporter*. Thanks are in order to the editors of these publications for permission to reprint.

Sources

Chapter One: The Taming of American Politics

The nearest thing to a textbook on supermarket politics is offered by James M. Cannon, ed., *Politics U.S.A.* (New York, 1960), which contains contributions from the more practical politicians. The quotation from Murray Chotiner is taken from this source, as is John F. Kennedy's observation on candidates and brand names. Stanley Kelley's *Professional Public Relations and Political Power* (Baltimore, 1956) is a useful specialized study; it yielded the remark by Clem Whitaker which heads the chapter. Gordon Cotler's "That Plague of Spots from Madison Avenue," in *The Reporter*, November 25, 1952, was a pioneering effort and contains Rosser Reeves's piquant observations. I have relied in part on Daniel Seligman's "The New Masses," *Fortune*, May, 1959, for data on the social setting. The rest is from newspapers and periodicals, including Robert Kennedy's allusion to U.S. Steel (*Time*, August 8, 1960), and John F. Kennedy's statement on the mechanics of politics (*Time*, November 7, 1960). A television set, of course, is an indispensable additional tool of research.

Chapter Two: Washington: Leviathan, Inc.

For the material on the Organization Bureaucrat, I am indebted to Mrs. Beth Brod's quarrying. Since the Capitol, and those writing machines, nominally belong to the taxpayers, the rest is available to anybody with sturdy legs and stubborn curiosity. The quotation from Joseph and Stewart Alsop is from *The Reporter's Trade* (New York, 1958), and James Truitt's comments are from an article in the Washington *Post* of October 23, 1960. Newman's remark, which opens the chapter, appeared in *Idea of a University*, Discourse VI; my attention was drawn to it by Richard Hoggart's admirable *Uses of Literacy* (Fair Lawn, N. J., 1957), which should have been a best seller in Washington. It wasn't.

Chapter Three: The Coming of the Smooth Deal

A foreground view is presented by Samuel Lubell's two basic texts: *The Future of American Politics* (New York, 1952) and *Revolt of the Moderates* (New York, 1956); the latter provided the epigraph. I have consulted with profit the various case studies compiled by the Eagleton Foundation and published by Henry Holt & Co.; I have quoted John C. Donovan's monograph in the series, *Congressional Campaign: Maine Elects a Democrat* (1958). Richard Hofstadter's assessment of Bryan is from *The American Political Tradition* (New York, 1948), while Arthur M. Schlesinger's tribute to Stevenson can be found in *Kennedy or Nixon?* (New York, 1960).

Chapter Four: Suitors in the Cloakroom

President Kennedy's geriatric comment is quoted in Robert S. Allen and William V. Shannon, *The Truman*

Merry-Go-Round (New York, 1950). The Marquis Childs column appeared in the Washington *Post* of January 16, 1959, and Douglass Cater's survey of the tepid 86th was entitled "The Lonely Men on Capitol Hill," in *The Reporter*, October 15, 1959. The several quotations from Woodrow Wilson have been gathered from August Heckscher, ed., *The Politics of Woodrow Wilson* (New York, 1956), and from the paperback reissue of the classic *Congressional Government* (New York, 1956). The material on LaGuardia is from Howard Zin, *LaGuardia in Congress* (Ithaca, 1959) and Arthur M. Schlesinger, Jr., *The Crisis of the Old Order* (Boston, 1957). For further material on the Liberal Project, see the author's "Freshmen Ferment in an Old House," *Progressive*, July, 1960. The files of I. F. Stone's *Weekly* contain a hellbox of intriguing items on the trespasses of Congress; I have quoted from the September 5, 1960 issue of his invariably lively newsletter. I am grateful to Ralph Huitt of the University of Wisconsin for discussing some of the ideas developed in this chapter.

Chapter Five: Texas Leaves Its Landmarks

Elsie Carper of the Washington *Post*, who surely ranks as unofficial historian of the Battle of the East Front, very kindly made her files available to me. For a learned debate on this project, see the *Journal of the American Institute of Architects* of June, 1958. The rest is embalmed in newspaper morgues, except for the apt quotation from Petronius which appears in the William Arrowsmith translation of the *Satyricon* (New York, 1960, paperback ed.).

Chapter Six: *That Image in the White House*

In belles-lettres, there is an impressive body of lofty criticism of imagery; in politics, the field is wide open. However, the curious can consult, as did the author, Vance Packard's *Hidden Persuaders* (New York, 1957); John G. Schneider's " '56: Show-Bix Flop," *The Nation*, November 24, 1956; and William Lee Miller's "Can Government Be Merchandized?" *The Reporter*, October 27, 1953. The passage from Plato, of course, is in the Jowett rendering of *The Republic*, Book VII.

Chapter Seven: *Fortress of Yesterday*

Edmund Wilson's comment on the Supreme Court can be found in his *American Earthquake* (New York, 1959). I have also profited from the late Justice Robert H. Jackson's *The Struggle for Judicial Supremacy* (New York, 1941); Alpheus T. Mason's *The Supreme Court; From Taft to Warren* (Baton Rouge, 1958); and from *Nine Old Men* by Drew Pearson and Robert S. Allen, two journalists with injudicial temperament.

Chapter Eight: *The Soothing Cassandras*

The files of the *Nieman Reports* constitute a rich granary of information on the press. I have benefited, too, from Douglass Cater's *The Fourth Branch of Government* (New York, 1959), a lucid analysis of Washington jour-

nalism from which I have drawn the quotation that
heads the chapter. The remark by Louis M. Lyons is
from his article "Chain-Store Journalism," in *The Reporter*, December 8, 1960. As for the rest, it was snipped
with shears from the best newspapers.

Chapter Nine: From Melting Pot to Pressure Cooker

For general perspective, I have relied on John Higham's
Strangers in the Land (New Brunswick, 1955). Other
quotations were taken from John C. Miller, *Crisis in
Freedom* (Boston, 1952); Harry Barnard, *Eagle Forgotten*
(New York, 1938); and two yellowing nativist tracts,
Frederick R. Anspach, *Sons of the Sires* (Philadelphia,
1855) and Henry Davis Winters, *The Origin . . . of
the American Party* (1855). The comment by Randolph
Bourne is in his *History of a Literary Radical* (New York,
1956), where I was led by the omnibibliophilic Dwight
Macdonald. The author's doctoral thesis, *The Politics
of Loyalty: From La Follette to McCarthy in Wisconsin*
(1956), which is decently interred in the Princeton University Library, contains detailed data on ethnic patterns
in that state's voting.

Chapter Ten: The Twilight of Regionalism

Reverend Morse is quoted in Merrill Jensen, ed., *Regionalism in America* (Madison, 1951). I came upon
Congressman Maynard's lament in Carl Sandburg, *Abraham Lincoln: The War Years* (New York, 1939), Vol. I,

while John F. Kennedy used the Whitman philippic in a contribution to John M. Cannon, ed., *Politics U.S.A.* (New York, 1960). The Cannon volume also contains Leonard Hall's observations on TV in politics. Frederic Cassidy's "Dialect and Children's Games" is in the *Publication of the American Dialect Society* for April, 1958; and Jesse Stuart's "America's Last Carbon Copy" is in the *Saturday Review*, December 28, 1957.

Chapter Eleven: The Old in Heart

There are as many books and articles on what is wrong with youth as there are youngsters to scold. I did profit, however, from a series of articles on this theme published in the *New Leader* during 1957; the quotation from Wallace Markfield is from his contribution in the March 18 issue. Two Luce surveys were helpful: "The Class of '49," *Fortune*, June, 1949; and "The No-Nonsense Kids," *Time*, November 18, 1957. Concerning the Beats, I have drawn from Seymour Krim, ed., *The Beats* (New York, 1960, paperback, of course), in which there are contributions by Norman Podhoretz and John Clellon Holmes. The credo of the unidentified Beat is from Eugene Burdick, "The Innocent Nihilists Adrift in Squaresville," *The Reporter*, April 13, 1958. The fiery YAFF manifesto can be found in the *National Review*, November 24, 1960; and Dan Wakefield's searching profile, "William F. Buckley, Jr.: Portrait of a Complainer," is in the January, 1961 issue of *Esquire*. Dwight Macdonald dissects Buckleyism in his *Memoirs of a Revolutionist* (New York, 1957).

Chapter Twelve: Bohemia Moves Uptown

The quotation from Cyril Connolly is from *Enemies of Promise* (New York, 1960, paperback ed.). For material on Bohemia past, I have relied upon: Granville Hicks, *John Reed* (New York, 1936); Russell Lynes, *The Tastemakers* (New York, 1955); Thomas Craven, *Modern Art* (New York, 1934); Allen Churchill, *The Improper Bohemians* (New York, 1958). The remarks on little magazines are from Malcolm Cowley, *The Literary Situation* (New York, 1954); and William Barrett, "The Declining Fortunes of the Literary Review," *Anchor Review No. 2* (New York, 1957). Secretary Rusk is quoted by Dwight Macdonald, *The Ford Foundation* (New York, 1956), and I have benefited from the same author's "Masscult and Midcult" in the Summer and Fall issues of the *Partisan Review* in 1960. *Time's* organ tones sounded in the June 11, 1956 issue, for which Dr. Barzun, who is on the cover, bears no responsibility.

Chapter Thirteen: Who Killed the Bull Moose?

A useful compendium on third parties is in William B. Hesseltine's *The Rise and Fall of Third Parties* (Washington, 1948). Norman Thomas' anecdote is in his article, "Republicans and Democrats Are Stealing From My Socialist Platform," *Look*, August 17, 1948. The bulkiest autopsy on American socialism is the two-volume *Socialism in American Life* (Princeton, 1952), edited by D. D. Egbert and Stow Persons, from which I have taken quotations by Wilbur Moore and Daniel Bell. I have delved, with pleasure, in both Oscar Ameringer's *If You Don't Weaken* (New York, 1940) and Ralph Chaplin's *Wobbly* (Chicago, 1948). Mr. Romney's closing remark is quoted in Tom Mahoney, *The Story of George Romney* (New York, 1958), and the epigram from Laski which opens the chapter is from *Liberty and the Modern State* (New York, 1949).

Chapter Fourteen: Signposts to Futopia

Mr. Kronenberger's mordant complaint is quoted in *Look*, May 17, 1954. Besides Orwell and Huxley, a basic Futopian bookshelf ought to contain Eugene Zamiatin, *We* (New York, 1959, paperback ed.); Karel Capek, *War With the Newts* (New York, 1595, paperback ed.); Kurt Vonnegut, *Player Piano* (New York, 1952); Ray Bradbury, *Fahrenheit 451* (New York, 1953, paperback); David Karp, *One* (New York, 1953); Bernard Wolfe, *Limbo* (New York, 1952); Frederik Pohl and C. M. Kornbluth, *The Space Merchants* (New York, 1953, paperback); Isaac Asimov, *Nine Tomorrows* (New York, 1959); and Gore Vidal, *Messiah* (New York, 1954). I would also include B. F. Skinner, *Walden Two* (New York, 1948), except that the author, a Harvard behaviorist psychologist, explicitly informed me that he regards his vision of engineered virtue as benign. Other sources quoted include H. G. Wells, *Experiment in Autobiography* (New York, 1934) and *The Mind at the End of Its Tether* (London, 1945); Denis Gabor, "Inventing the Future," *Encounter*, May, 1960; and Thomas B. Morgan, "The People Machine," *Harper's*, January, 1961. The best anthology of the pre-Futopian literature is Glenn Negley and J. Max Patrick, eds., *The Quest for Utopia* (New York, 1952).

Chapter Fifteen: The Two Worlds

Mr. Stevenson's statement is in his article, "Putting First Things First," in *Foreign Affairs*, January, 1960. I came upon R. H. S. Crossman's observations in *The Charm of Politics* (New York, 1958), and in his article, "German Socialism Goes Democrat," *New Statesman*, December 3, 1960. The Steiner article was entitled "The Decline of the Labour Party" and appeared in the September 29, 1960 issue of *The Reporter*.

Afterword: The Sweet Smell of Excess

The Whitehead epigram was recorded in Lucien Price, *Dialogues of Alfred North Whitehead* (Boston, 1954). For more scholarly statements of this chapter's theme, see Dennis H. Wrong, "The Perils of Political Moderation," *Commentary*, January, 1959; and John Higham, "The Cult of the 'American Consensus,'" *Commentary*, February, 1959. See also John F. Kennedy, *Profiles in Courage* (New York, 1956).

Index of Names